EARLE BIRNEY

STUDIES IN CANADIAN LITERATURE

General Editors: Hugo McPherson, Gary Geddes

EARLE BIRNEY

Frank Davey

The Copp Clark Publishing Company

The author is an Assistant Professor of English at York University, Toronto. He has founded and edited two literary magazines, *Tish* and *The Open Letter*, and is the author of several books, among which are *Weeds* and *Four Myths for Sam Perry*.

© Copyright Canada 1971 by
The Copp Clark Publishing Company.
Printed and bound in Canada

CONTENTS

ACKNOWLEDGEMENTS

Excerpts from *Chaucer's Irony, David and Other Poems, Now Is Time, The Strait of Anian,* and *Trial of a City and Other Verse* are reprinted with the kind permission of the author.

Excerpts from *The Creative Writer* are reprinted with the kind permission of CBC Publications.

Excerpts from *Down the Long Table, Ice Cod Bell or Stone, Near False Creek Mouth, Rag and Bone Shop, Selected Poems,* and *Turvey* are reprinted with the kind permission of The Canadian Publishers, McClelland and Stewart Limited, Toronto.

ABBREVIATIONS

The quotations from Birney's works are taken from the following editions.

CI *Chaucer's Irony*. Doctoral Dissertation. Toronto: University of Toronto, 1936.

CW *The Creative Writer*. Toronto: CBC Publications, 1966.

DLT *Down the Long Table*. Toronto: McClelland and Stewart, 1955.

DOP *David and Other Poems*. Toronto: Ryerson, 1942.

ICBS *Ice Cod Bell or Stone*. Toronto: McClelland and Stewart, 1962.

NFCM *Near False Creek Mouth*. Toronto: McClelland and Stewart, 1964.

NIT *Now Is Time*. Toronto: Ryerson, 1945.

RBS *Rag and Bone Shop*. Toronto: McClelland and Stewart, 1971.

SA *The Strait of Anian*. Toronto: Ryerson, 1948.

SP *Selected Poems*. Toronto: McClelland and Stewart, 1966.

T *Turvey*. Toronto: McClelland and Stewart, 1949.

TC *Trial of a City and Other Verse*. Toronto: Ryerson, 1952.

THE CAREER

It is the anomalies which give Earle Birney's career its shape and character. He was born, Friday May 13th, 1904, in Calgary, at that time part of the Northwest Territories, where his family home was a log cabin on the banks of the Bow River. From infancy to seven years he lived in northern Alberta on a remote and primitive farm two miles from neighbours and fifteen miles from town. Thirty-two years later he was teaching at University College, University of Toronto, although neither of his parents had completed even elementary school education. Before 1921, Birney himself expected to remain for life a labourer. However in 1922, when he enrolled at the University of British Columbia, his ambition was to be a chemical engineer. In the thirties, while working at his doctorate, his principal concern was not his Chaucerian studies, but Marxism. In the late forties and early fifties, when he had won two Governor-General's awards for poetry and was busy publishing two novels and two further books of verse, his principal concern was not his writing, but his teaching and Chaucerian studies. And, until his retirement from full-time teaching in 1965, he regarded himself as a "Sunday" writer; his commitment to be principally a poet occurred only after he was sixty-one years of age.

Yet despite preventing in Birney what might have

been a concerted push toward a writing career, these anomalies permitted him a rich and complex life which informs all of his writing. As a child he lived without playmates or siblings in the now almost vanished Canadian wilderness. On leaving high school he spent a winter working on one of Canada's first mosquito-control projects. In 1934, while an instructor at the Mormon-administrated University of Utah, he was suspended for Marxist activities, but was rehired as a result of an unprecedented student general strike. In 1934 and 1935, he was a Trotskyist functionary in England, at work reconciling various factions of the party and organizing a party cell within the Independent Labour Party. He interviewed Trotsky in Norway and was jailed briefly in Germany for failing to salute a Nazi parade. From 1936 to 1940 he was literary editor of the *Canadian Forum*, from 1942 to 1945 an officer in the Canadian Army, and during 1946 and 1947 head of the Canadian Broadcasting Corporation's international short-wave broadcast service.

The fact that Birney was for the greater part of his writing career merely a "Sunday" writer, not only in the sense of the time which he gave to writing, but also in the importance that he attributed to it, makes a study of his biography more relevant to his work than it might otherwise have been. Birney began concentrated efforts to write only at thirty-six years of age. Thus, his formative years embraced not only his childhood and youth, but also a busy decade of his maturity. When he did take up writing with sufficient seriousness to put forth verse collections and novels, it was a secondary activity, coloured and jostled by all too many other activities to which Birney chose to give his hours. Like most men, Birney was pursued inexorably though not maliciously by the consequences of commitments and actions.

From birth to 1922 he led a strictly rural life. The Lacombe farm which his parents bought during his infancy was uncleared and unpaying; his father spent his winters working in Calgary or Lethbridge, leaving young Birney and his mother to feed the stock. The only neighbours were a Métis and a German-speaking family neither of which had any significant contact with the Birneys. Birney recalls himself here as a "Wordsworthian child," necessarily spending long solitary hours near the woods and stream beside the farmhouse. This enforced solitude seems also to have contributed to his learning to read at a very early age—newspapers, the Bible, *Livingstone in Darkest Africa*, *Pilgrim's Progress*, all before his family's move to Banff in 1911. On Sundays, his mother took him into Morningside where she taught Sunday School. They stayed the entire day there, having dinner with the parson and attending the evening service. On these occasions Birney made his only contacts with other children and borrowed books to read during the rest of the week.

Even at this time his parents were extremely interested in their only son's education. While neither of them was well educated, both were wise enough to see the economic value of learning. His mother was an extraordinarily devout woman from an impoverished fishing family in the Shetland Islands who had left Scotland as a young girl to find work as a chambermaid in Canada. Her portrait finds its way into Birney's "Joe Harris, 1913-1942."

She is proud and fair still in the scratched wedding

3

picture, proud of my straight-eyed father, I think, and proud of the trail travelled; from the whipped brood of a drunken fisherman, lost on the elbow of God on the North Sea; from the servant's cell of a Glasgow snob; from the spattered kitchen of a miner's hotel in the Kootenays.

I remember her first when she stood in the ranch door, her eyes like garnets, the coils of her hair golden above the butt of the shotgun, while the crazy half-breed zigzagged back through the scrub by the creek. (SP, 83)

His father had run away from his Guelph, Ontario home at fifteen years of age in 1880, found work driving horses from Chicago to Calgary, and remained in the west. Shortly after arriving in Calgary he had yielded to his parents' wishes, and apprenticed as a painter and paper hanger; however, he afterward had held a succession of frontier jobs, hunting fossils for an American museum, working on the ferries in San Francisco, and prospecting (again on behalf of U.S. interests) for silver from northern California to northern Alberta. He had become in fact, a sort of itinerant international westerner, for twenty years taking most of western North America for his territory.

But the parents were never to prosper. They had met in Rossland, British Columbia in 1899, and married shortly thereafter. On Earle's birth in 1904 the father turned to farming as more suitable for a family man than prospecting, but the Lacombe farm was rocky, wooded, and unproductive. In 1911, the father sold the farm and moved the family to Banff so that Earle could be close to

4

a school. The boy now encountered a host of new books —novels by Henty, Scott, Dumas, and Captain Marryatt, the nature stories of Charles G. D. Roberts, as well as many lesser works of youthful romanticism. Here the father worked at painting and paper hanging until 1915, when he left to fight in World War I. He returned in 1916 shell-shocked and rheumatic, physically incapable of resuming his trade. Veterans assistance funds helped him to purchase a farm near Creston, British Columbia, but there he found not only the soil poor but water scarce.

Birney recalls that throughout his childhood his family had to struggle for economic survival. Although his father was an "old fashioned journeyman" and suspicious of unionism, and in addition a strong supporter of the Imperial British Empire, he was apparently outspoken in his belief that the Canadian working man was being short-changed. Perhaps because of his experiences in working and prospecting for American employers, he blamed the misfortunes of the Canadian working class solely on U.S. exploitation. Many years later in his son's work, attacks on both capitalism and American vulgarities become commonplace. But although money was scarce, the family's stress on education never wavered. Books and newspapers were plentiful at all times. Both parents urged Birney to excel at learning, the father wishing that he thus seek economic security, and the mother that he qualify as a missionary. Both seem also to have over-protected him, at no time allowing him to own a gun or operate a trap line, but instead committing him until far into his teens to play the organ at church services. Birney remembers that as a result he often wished to leave high school merely to spite them, and nearly decided not to attend university because they were urging him to. However, two years of casual labour after high school—as a fifteen-dollar-a-week bank teller, cucumber picker, pick-and-shovel worker, capped by a job on a mosquito-control party directed by a university graduate—finally convinced Birney of the economic value of education, and he enrolled at the University of British Columbia in the fall of 1922. Some indication of his parents' interest in him is provided by their abruptly moving from Banff (they had sold the Creston farm a little more than a year before) to Vancouver later that year.

Thus Birney's university career began in economic self-interest, and was maintained by this through most of the succeeding years. Birney's goal then was to rise from common labourer to the level of his former superiors in his many Rocky Mountain jobs. As a freshman he hoped to become a chemical engineer; as a sophomore (after a year of shattered laboratory glassware) to be a geologist. But during the sophomore year his interest in reading which had begun in the isolation of the Lacombe farm led him to take an additional English course—from the charismatic chairman of the department, Garnett Sedgewick. That year saw Birney appointed associate editor of the campus newspaper, *The Ubyssey*, saw him publish in that paper his first poems (Elizabethan-style sonnets) and commit himself to the English honours program. Between his third and fourth years he was appointed editor-in-chief of the *Ubyssey*, and consequently offered a summer job as editor of the *Point Grey Gazette*, then owned by the reeve of Point Grey municipality. In light of Birney's later political activities, this job seems significant. Says Birney, "That was the year I learned some of the normal corruption of city life." The reeve instructed him to put on the front page only municipal news that flattered him, and to restrict publicity on the society page to events that concerned his supporters. Meanwhile, the reeve himself pressured full-page ads from "people who were bidding for large contracts—street-paving, pipe-laying—in Point Grey."[1] Birney earned several thousand dollars that summer. In the following year, as editor of the *Ubyssey*, he spearheaded two campaigns, one to stop American football on campus and the second to prevent the University from accepting the gift of a gymnasium from the Department of National Defence in exchange for doubled student enlistment in the officer training corps. For the latter campaign both the newspaper and his editorship were suspended by the University president, though not before Birney had clandestinely published in advance the last scheduled issue of the year.

Despite the time he gave to the *Ubyssey* and its various causes, Birney graduated that spring (1926) with First Class Honours. He was offered fellowships for graduate study by both the University of California at Berkeley and the University of Toronto. For the next six years he devoted himself entirely to study and to teaching. He received his M.A. from the University of Toronto in 1927, and, when Toronto could not find money to help him further, went on to Berkeley to begin the doctorate. His three years of study there under such distinguished scholars as Merrett Hughes, Arthur Brodeur, and John Tatlock, ended abruptly when the English department split into rival Yale and Harvard factions. When the Harvard faction became dominant, Birney's projected dissertation, which had been planned under the guidance of Hughes of the Yale faction, was abruptly termed by Tatlock unsatisfactory due to its broad working definition of irony. Birney refused to alter this definition, and by the fall of 1930 the department had found him an instructorship at the University of Utah and barred him permanently from completing his program. He taught in Utah for two years before managing to transfer his Berkeley credits to the University of Toronto and secure fellowship assistance there.

Had he managed to complete the Berkeley doctorate, it seems likely that by 1931 Birney would have become a medievalist at an American university. Given the reputation of the Berkeley degree and the stature of his supervisors, he could have become a highly successful one. But while conflicts within the Berkeley faculty may have stunted a promising academic career, they indirectly led to what was probably Birney's most crucial year: 1932-33. Officially, it was a year in residence to qualify for the Toronto Ph.D.; in fact, it became a year-long immersion in Canada's political underworld.

It was now twelve years since he had left high school. Throughout this time, with the exception of his years at Utah, he had lived on casual earnings and on fellowships. Twice he had been engaged to be married, but both weddings had been fatally scheduled in the never-never land of financial security. He recalls that it seemed as if the depression had lasted since his high school graduation, and moreover, as if there had never been a time when his family had not had to struggle to live. Always a humanitarian, in the fall of 1932 Birney began to believe that he was probably a socialist and to inquire, in a somewhat humorous and naïve way, into what socialism was. He went to both Lorne Morgan and Harold Cassidy of the University of Toronto for guidance, receiving Marxist literature from the former and Social Democratic literature from the latter. Within hours of reading the *Communist Manifesto*, Birney was convinced he was a Marxist. At a party at Cassidy's the young poetess Dorothy Livesay introduced him to the Communist youth leaders on campus, Jean Watts and Stanley Ryerson. For a brief time he attempted to join them, but they were highly suspicious of so easy and intellectual a convert. Then one evening at another Cassidy party, Birney began arguing with Watts and Ryerson over Stalin's teaching that Social Democrats were more dangerous than Nazis. An attractive young girl who clearly knew every nuance and faction of International Communism came to his rescue. She turned out to be a Trotskyist youth leader, and Birney quickly grew to believe both that he was in love with her and that he was truly a Trotskyist. He nursed the latter illusion for seven years.

For the remainder of 1932-33, Birney devoted himself to learning to be a good Trotskyist and to courting Sylvia Johnstone. Secondarily, he completed his course work at the University. In the spring of 1933, the Trotskyist group decided that he would serve the party best by returning to his job in Utah (thus earning money for the cause) and by organizing left-wing protest there. Accordingly, he left for Utah via Vancouver (where he was to teach summer school at the University of British Columbia) in the company of Sylvia. On arrival in Salt Lake City they married, largely to appease the Roman Catholic side of Sylvia's only superficially Marxist mother. However, their relationship had for several months been marred by Sylvia's illness and homesickness. Immediately after the wedding she left for Toronto to attempt to resolve these. She did not return, and the marriage was annulled in 1936.

In Utah, the effects of the depression in the traditionally conservative Mormon state provided Birney with many opportunities for action. Union leaders were being kidnapped by night riders. News of disputes between labour groups and the state government was being suppressed by the newspapers. In the coal mines of Carbon County, striking miners were being pressured back to work by the imposition of martial law. Birney worked chiefly to publicize cases of persecution and to arrange for left-wing leaders to speak in Salt Lake City. His most adventurous act was to help chaperone a group of students who made an unauthorized entry into Carbon County to investigate conditions. Birney's account of this expedition ("Utah Students see for Themselves") was published in the *Student Review* (February, 1934) under the pseudonym David Brownstone. The relationship he perceived at this time between literature and politics is indicated in an unpublished book review he wrote for the *Utah Chronicle*, the University's student newspaper.

The main stream of true world literature today is already beginning to flow into the channels graved by John Dos Passos and Henri Barbusse and André Gide. These are men who know that the class struggle participates in you, if you won't in it, and that the real mastery of your artist's fate comes with *conscious* enrollment and not on the side of Capitalism. That will

10

not hurt your "art" . . . ; but it will make clear and strong your voices.

. . . in the exploited lives of our citizen majority across the tracks and under the wires, in the mines of Carbon Country and the Logan beet fields, in factory, store, office and—yes—even in the University, in the struggle of all who work with hand or head to free our world from wage slavery and its buddy The Profit System, lies the shining challenge for all who would write mightily today![2]

By 1934, chiefly because of the Carbon County expedition which would have earned him permanent suspension by the University except for the student general strike on his behalf, Birney was no longer welcome at Utah. By chance, Pelham Edgar, his director at the University of Toronto, obtained a fellowship for him to study in England and complete his dissertation. That fall, after teaching at the University of British Columbia's summer session as he had each summer since 1928, Birney shipped out from Port Alberni as an ordinary seaman on a British freighter. He had managed to contact the Trotskyist hierarchy in Europe before leaving, and had received instructions to join the party faction within the British Independent Labour Party. He was also instructed to attempt to reconcile this faction with two other self-proclaimed groups of Trotskyists in England. Throughout 1935, he spent his nights and weekends organizing unemployed groups for the I.L.P., travelling to Cardiff, Liverpool, Glasgow, and most of the midland industrial cities. In London, he lived in a central but poor area off Theobald's Road; while travelling he often had to sleep on the flagstone corridor of a rat-infested tenement, or (preferably) on the wooden benches of meeting halls. When the 1935 British elections were held, Birney was used by the I.L.P. to campaign for the Labour Party against the Mosleyites in a constituency where the I.L.P. had no candidate. This was a more time-consuming activity than it might at first appear, since roving gangs of Black Shirts in armoured trucks continually attacked I.L.P. speakers and forced them into the tactic of giving innumerable brief hit-and-run speeches from the roofs of automobiles. Through his political work he met Esther Bull, a member of one of the renegade Trotskyist factions, whom he not only converted to the official party line but brought to Canada and married shortly before World War II.

In his free time, chiefly on weekdays, Birney worked in the British Museum on his dissertation, which he completed shortly before leaving England in February, 1936. Entitled *Chaucer's Irony*, it is a two volume work that consists chiefly of an annotated index to every instance of verbal and dramatic irony in Chaucer that Birney could detect. It is a meticulously documented but poorly organized example of dissertation overkill. While its thesis makes interesting reading, its review of past criticism seems an irrelevant and mandatory exercise. The annotated listing of ironies, which provides the supporting evidence for the thesis, is completely isolated from the rest of the work and thus reads like a book-length footnote. Thesis and evidence come together only in the concluding pages.

The dissertation had begun in the 1926 Honours

Essay Birney had written at the University of British Columbia for Garnett Sedgewick. Throughout his doctoral studies at Berkeley he had added to the catalogue of ironies and groped to give this catalogue a justifiable purpose. The work had remained unfocused until his Marxist conversion; then a thesis emerged:

> . . . the direct influence upon Chaucer's literary expression of the ambiguous class-position in which Chaucer found himself, his middle-class origins, his courtly connections, his responsive interest in the new vigorous world of the bourgeois, and his economic and social need to reconcile that interest with the duties of a courtier. It is with a discussion and exemplification of this life-long contradiction in Chaucer, and its resulting literary irony, that much of the present study will be concerned. (*CI*, I, 55)

Basic to the dissertation was Birney's repudiation of the "work of art as a unique and static experience." Instead, he based his argument on "the concept that history, or at least the history of great art, is basically affected by such 'common or garden' things as the way by which the artist secured food, clothing and shelter for himself" (*CI*, V, 22). He began by defining irony as "unavoidably satiric, subtle, moral, mimic, and snobbish, . . ." as "appealing primarily to bourgeois appraisers of literature, to those who believe or encourage the myth of the lone artist's 'impartiality,' and glorify the presentation of the individual opposed to the masses" (*CI*, I, 42-43). He further defined it as "punch-pulling":

13

> Punch-pulling may become a habit, a life-attitude
> like the *sophrosyne*, the 'passion for moderation,' with
> which Thomson credits Erasmus. For this again is
> part and parcel of class doctrines, of the gentlemanly
> traditions which expect the artist to remain 'above' the
> struggles of his day, . . . (*CI*, I, 45)

Then the faint invectives draw Birney away from the
declared topic of his investigation.

> The trend of the thirties, however, is to abandon the
> ivory tower, and to weld literature with the need for
> direct, rapid, and intensely constructive social action.
> Art is entering, perhaps, into a whole world of new
> standards, and of desires beyond negativism. Changing
> material conditions bring new needs and new ideolo-
> gies to meet them. A world in crisis absorbs its artists
> too in a partisan consideration of humanism, fascism,
> communism, Anglo-Catholicism; such prominent writ-
> ers as Gide and Barbusse, Dos Passos, and even, in a
> different way, T. S. Eliot and Chesterton, seek not to
> preserve poise and individuality so much, as to co-
> ordinate their art actively with social reform. Irony, in
> contemporary values, becomes, by contrast, the escape
> of the weak or overcautious. (*CI*, I, 46-47)

These irrelevant passages with their implied criticism of
Chaucer for not being someone else, are not frequent in
the work, but occur often enough to give it a decidedly
equivocal tone. On the one hand, Birney's scholarly
training brings him to pay tribute to Chaucer's "rhythmic
grace and posed nuance of phrase, . . . the ever-open eye

and mind and heart of this greatest of all English humorists" (*CI*, VI, 170). And on the other hand, his Marxism leads him to group Chaucer with Anatole France in their sharing "irony as . . . a mode of escape from, or at least of compromise with, the fundamental problems which confront the thinker in the life of his day" (*CI*, IV, 12), and to condemn them jointly:

> . . . in both there was perhaps a refusal to 'grow up,' a refusal which, however unavoidable it might have been and however charming the literary results, yet is just sufficient to exclude them from the circle which the world preserves for its very greatest. (*CI*, IV, 32)

The major flaw of this work, aside from its structural problems is surely the relationship Birney tends to perceive between political courage and literary merit. He cannot dispel the impression of preferring outspoken courage without literary value to artistic work based on equivocal statements. Remarks such as, "one cannot give one's highest praise to the artist whose technique we admire but whose thought we must admit to be just a little trivial" (*CI*, IV, 12-13) leave the reader to wonder just what Birney would give to such an artist, and elsewhere he doesn't say. Birney serves two masters throughout the dissertation, and of course cannot serve both equally well. A year later he advises readers of the Trotskyist journal, *The Link,* to curb their literary interests:

> I would . . . not allow my reading of *proletarian* literature to interfere with the much bigger job of helping

to organize my fellow workers towards the establishment of a society where writers will be free to express themselves without starving or turning intellectual traitors.[3]

Would he have called Chaucer an "intellectual traitor"? In 1936, and in a Trotskyist context it would not have been impossible.

Divided loyalties continue to bedevil Birney's career. The anomalies at the beginning of this chapter are symptomatic of them. Country versus city, western Canada versus eastern Canada, worker versus bourgeois, revolution versus establishment, and eventually, poet versus academician. In 1936, the year in which Birney takes both a faculty appointment at the University of Toronto and literary editorship of the left-of-center *Canadian Forum*, his conflict of loyalties is clearly preserved in *Chaucer's Irony*, where an extraordinarily conservative formalism of structure co-exists with a diatribe against "good form," against impartiality, and against academic "aloofness" and objectivity. Birney's career begins to be characterized by compromise, an action which he consistently decried in Chaucer. In his dissertation, literary judgement becomes subordinate to political judgement. In his life, Marxist revolutionary hopes are supported by bourgeois professional employment. As in 1933, the Trotskyists decide that he is of more value to them as a salaried employee than as a free-lance revolutionary, and advise him to accept the University of Toronto post. Consequently, 1935's Trotskyist organizer of England becomes 1936's junior instructor, teaching freshman, sophomore and honours courses, and graduate seminars

16

simultaneously, and having little time for work with the party.

A lesser compromise was involved in Birney's assumption of the *Canadian Forum* post. While its editors were Social Democrats, the journal itself presented a wide range of left-wing opinion from the radicalism of young David Lewis to the theoretical purity of Lorne Morgan. Birney's articles and reviews throughout 1937 and 1938 are uncompromisingly Trotskyist. His subjects are nearly always left-wing writers and his complaints about them invariably concern their Stalinist leanings. In addition he writes under the pen-name "Rufus" a monthly news column, "Another Month," a highly selective listing of instances of capitalist greed and Stalinist hypocrisy.

Christmas gifts include an ivory-framed portrait of George V and Mary (from mamma to son Edward), a consignment of German gas masks on credit (from a Hungarian Burgomaster to his staff), fourteen billion dollars worth of armaments (from the world to the world).

Albertan farmer's three children found starving without blankets, with pneumonia . . . Toronto store reports great Christmas demand for $120 nightgowns.

Caretaker for Diego Rivera, world's foremost communist mural painter, is beaten up by Stalinites because Diego gives shelter to foremost communist thinker and Red Army founder, Leon Trotsky.[4]

But by 1938 Rufus has been replaced by a less strident

member of the *Forum* staff, Rufus II, and when war breaks out Birney's own reviews become less politically doctrinaire, more literary, and his occasional articles ("To Arms with Canadian Poetry," "War and the English Intellectuals") more objective.

These years, 1936 to 1941, at the *Canadian Forum* are important ones artistically for Birney. In this period he publishes his first mature poem, "Slug in Woods," his best known poem, "David," and compiles the manuscript of his first book of verse. He begins as a literary unknown but within six years wins a Governor-General's award. He begins this period as a Marxist, but ends it—and remains—disillusioned and politically non-affiliated. And he begins it as an occasional and amateur sonneteer and ends it as a recognized professional poet. The fact is that, counter to Milton Wilson's view,[5] Birney is poetically a late-starter; although he attempts poems as early as 1920, his serious engagement with poetry begins late in his Marxist period while literary editor of the *Canadian Forum*.

The nature of his interests in this period has a profound effect on his later work. Both the humanitarianism which led Birney to Marxism and the optimistic humanism of Marxism itself endure throughout his poetry in the underlying assumption that poetry should speak to men and assist them to master their circumstances. More particularly, Birney's Marxism serves to limit his literary curiosity and experiences, to give him only a partial view of contemporary writing. Throughout his *Canadian Forum* years, while he reviews Canadian poetry with catholicity, his taste in non-Canadian literature is selective. His preferences run to fiction, particularly to that of Faulkner, Farrell, Steinbeck, Dreiser and Anderson. In poetry his interest is chiefly in John Lehmann's New Writing Anthologies and in the leading British Marxists.

I think in the mid-thirties I read a great deal of Auden, Spender, Lewis; I did not read an equivalent amount of the Americans at that time, and this was bad for me in developing contemporaneity, because Auden, Spender, Lewis were not really contemporary in the way that Pound was or many people.

I was more hung up on the Auden tradition because it was Marxist. . . . (Interview, October 26, 1969)

On the other hand, Birney reviews both Joyce's *Finnigan's Wake* and Gertrude Stein's *Ida* in this period and finds both uninteresting; he terms Miss Stein "the greatest bore among the modern writers."[6] In short, and as one might have guessed from his politics, Birney in the late thirties prefers the writers concerned with ideas to those concerned with form and language. This preference will eventually lead to Munro Beattie's unjust accusation that he "never quite succeeded in making poetry" of his "worry about the world."[7] More immediately it will lead to Birney's being his own instructor in matters of form, often borrowing in the first three books, and experimenting frequently with Cummingsesque ploys in the later ones. Throughout his career Birney will not often be a leader in poetic technique, but will instead take from whatever writers have come to his attention techniques that aid him in communicating—in the sixties even the techniques of concrete poetry.

The approach of war brought further important changes in Birney's career. Throughout 1938 and 1939 the statements of most political groups became shrill and confused; though now taking little part in most Trotskyist activities, Birney wrote many unsigned dogmatic pamphlets for the party—"Throw Kerensky into History's Ashcan"—almost all of which were destroyed at war's outbreak. In September, 1939, the Canadian government declared all Marxist literature and political statement illegal; most of his fellow Trotskyists deserted the party and Birney found himself the leading member of the remaining few. But when International Trotskyism supported the Soviet attack on Finland, Birney too deserted. Meanwhile, editorial opinion in the *Canadian Forum* moved considerably to the right, and Birney was released in 1940 as literary editor, although he continued to publish articles and reviews in the *Forum* through 1941. On Birney himself the coming of war had a powerful and significant effect, one which is only partly indicated by his poem, "Vancouver Lights." He was thirty-five years old, had made no major accomplishment, and the world with which he was familiar seemed to be disappearing completely and forever. Throughout the thirties he had seen himself "as a scholar, critic, Marxist, potential novelist," but not as a poet. Then, in 1939-40 he wrote "David," "Dusk on English Bay," "Vancouver Lights," "Anglosaxon Street," and most of the other poems of his first volume. He tells us of this time,

I was writing because I felt, dammit, I wanted to say this kind of thing, I wanted to do this kind of thing, or see if I could do it, for a long time, and now I see the war closing around me and I'm either going to go to jail or I'm going to go overseas, and don't know who's going to survive, or what.

In '39, as soon as war's declared, I began writing poems. (Interview, October 26, 1969)

In a 1946 interview Birney suggests that his becoming a poet was an even greater coincidence—that he would have preferred fiction.

I suppose the pressure of world events made me feel that there were things I wanted to say, and I didn't have time to say them in any lengthier way . . . poetry has been for me a safety valve . . . an opportunity for blowing off steam occasionally . . . a spare time occupation.[8]

At the invasion of Russia, Birney joined the Canadian Officer Training Corps at the University and obtained a reserve commission. In 1942, as soon as his contract with the University expired, he joined the active army, Personnel Selection Service. Although his duties kept him travelling while in Canada, and eventually sent him to England and Holland, the war brought him the most leisure time he had had since reaching adulthood. It was his first and longest sabbatical. Academic research and politics could no longer engage him, and after the war ended he had a second book of poems, *Now Is Time*, ready for publication. His war experiences are relevant chiefly to his novel *Turvey*, and are discussed in chapter two. What these experiences do not explain is the astonishing loss of political radicalism that occurs in him over these years. After the war he writes reviews and articles that have scarcely a breath of political content. Moreover, in 1946 he becomes, in effect, an agent of Canada's Department of External Affairs through his assuming the post of supervisor of foreign language broadcasts to Europe for the International Service of the Canadian Broadcasting Corporation. He tells us of this job, "I was responsible for making sure that the Canadian foreign policy was accurately reflected in the broadcasts I was in charge of" (Interview, October 26, 1969). A few years before, he had belonged to a group that dreamed of destroying both this foreign policy and its government. A similarly strange decision by Birney was his joining our country's most reactionary and self-congratulatory literary body, The Canadian Author's Association, and accepting the editorship of its *Canadian Poetry Magazine* (September 1946–June 1948). His letter of resignation[9] may damn the association, but only lamely explains his joining.

In September of 1947 he returns to both university teaching and the west coast, accepting an appointment at the University of British Columbia. He finds the University crowded with returning veterans, his lecture load high, and his salary sufficient to allow him to house his family in a rented army hut. Despite the eventual graduation of the veterans, Birney continued to find little time to write during his nineteen years at the University. His introduction of a creative writing program to the English department, while setting a precedent for Canada, further crowded his schedule when the department refused to consider it part of his teaching load. He claims to have in some years taught six courses: two creative writing, one freshman, one sophomore, a senior Chaucer course, and a graduate seminar. Birney appears to have squandered what little free time he did have during the academic year by writing popular-taste articles and radio talks in an effort to supplement his low salary. Articles such as, "Yes, Canadians can read—But Do They?,[10] "Mexico in One Jump,"[11] and radio talks such as "On Being a Canadian Author"[12] or the four talks which comprise *The Creative Writer* are no more than popular journalism. They are of transitory interest and written in the kind of dated colloquialism that can occur when a scholar tries to talk down to an audience—"hullabaloo," "what in tarnation," "doggerel and catterel" (in the 1966 publication, *The Creative Writer*). As in the thirties, Birney appears again to have lent his pen to a cause outside writing—here the popularization of literature and the few dollars it could earn him. At times money alone seems to have been sufficient to win him. Witness the following he wrote for a Standard Oil Company promotional photograph of Lake O'Hara.

Not on castle walls nor on the quilted farmlands and bridled lakes of older worlds falls this splendour. Here, tremulous with opal fire, the ceremony of dawn breathes down over summits older than story, over scars hewn by the endless besiegings of wind, of ice, of sun, and over battlements towered by the unimaginable power of the wrinkling globe itself.[13]

Yet throughout his period at the University of British Columbia, lack of time to write was his chief complaint. He did almost all of his serious work in summer or on sabbaticals: *Strait of Anian*, summer of 1947; *Turvey*, summer of 1948; *Trial of a City*, and several other radio plays, summers of 1949 to 1952; *Down the Long Table*, 1953, during a fellowship to France; *Ice Cod Bell or Stone*, 1958 and 1959, while holding a Nuffield Grant to do Chaucer research in England; *Near False Creek Mouth*, 1962 and 1963, while holding a Canada Council Grant to give a reading tour of Latin America. When asked by Al Purdy why he began teaching university, Birney remarked, "I took the way that I trained myself for—which was a teacher, but boy it sure mucked up my doing any more writing."[14] In another interview by Merilyn Evans he stated that the academy

> led me into ways of life which made it very difficult for me to write—I mean the quantity which I wanted to write. . . . For everything I've written I've had twenty things I've wanted to write. . . . This doesn't mean I'd have written any better, but on the other hand, I suspect it means I would have. If you write a lot you get better . . . if only better technically.[15]

In retrospect it seems clear that Birney was making definite choices at this time: the choice to be a university teacher, the choice to supplement his income by writing, the choice to limit his writing to a part-time activity. When asked to explain his self-image during the late forties and early fifties, he replied, "I thought of myself as a trained Chaucerian teacher, and as an inactive Chaucer scholar" (Interview, October 26, 1969). Again, not as a poet or writer. Elsewhere in this latter interview he stated that it was strained finances plus family respon-

24

sibilities that kept him teaching at the University of British Columbia and broadcasting for the CBC. Whether or not he knew better or eventually learned better is difficult to decide, but in 1966 he gave the following advice to the young writer:

If he cannot marry a wife able and willing to support him till he begins to make a living by his work . . . , the writer certainly should eschew the totally absorbing professions, even when they seem to be offering him a chance to write. The administrative staffs of our newspapers, advertising firms, and publishing houses, and of the CBC and the National Film Board, as well as of our high schools and universities are the present graveyards of most of Canada's once-possible literary artists.

My advice to young Canadian writers is, therefore, to take a temporary part-time job. (*CW*, 57-58)

What really happened to Birney and his career during the University of British Columbia years we may never know. One of the more illuminating comments he has made about them follows:

The big reason for my small publication as a writer, considering the number of years that I've lived, is a curious laziness. . . . My energy is often a screen against harder work. If I were sitting being quiet, thinking of that poem that is nagging, I would be working a hell of a lot harder. Instead, I'm running around giving poetry readings, or, doing anything, chopping trees down, going out to parties, all these things as a way of escaping that dreadful hard work that only seems to be. I find it very difficult to make the start . . . yet when I do it, then I get caught up in it and I don't want to do anything else till it's finished. (Interview, October 26, 1969)

Thus, perhaps, the sporadic appearance of Birney's books —poetry 1942, 1945, 1948, 1952, 1962, 1964, 1966, 1971; novels 1949 and 1955—and the large number of ephemeral and scholarly publications. The silence between *Down the Long Table* and *Ice Cod Bell or Stone* can be partly explained by the fact that during 1960 and 1961 Birney collected, collated, and edited the Malcolm Lowry manuscripts. Why he chose to do this rather than write, and what happened to the other years, Birney has tried to explain in this way:

I think there was a short period when I felt what the hell, you know. I didn't seem to be getting anywhere as a writer. Especially after *Down the Long Table* was a flop. (Interview, October 26, 1969)

Earle Birney did not make a full commitment to writing until 1965, the year of the publication of *Selected Poems*, when he left the University of British Columbia and became Writer-in-Residence at Scarborough College, University of Toronto. His years of frustration over both his workload and the status of creative writing at the University of British Columbia had been culminated by his advice being ignored in the formation of the new Department of Creative Writing, and by his being overlooked for its chairmanship. Since the Scarborough College post, the first of its type to be offered in Canada, he has been Writer-in-Residence at Massey College (1966-67) and at the University of Waterloo (1967-68). Lately, he has avoided any full-time academic employment, and devoted himself to travelling, giving readings and lectures, preparing an edition of Lowry poems, and writing.

Given the various facts of Birney's career, it is difficult to dismiss what Milton Wilson terms "the legend of Birney the late starter" and "the legend of a poetic hiatus in the mid-fifties."[16] While Birney's dating of poems in *Selected Poems* indicates a scattered attempt at poetry before 1939, there is no evidence that Birney took his own writing of verse seriously before that date. In addition, notes Birney has made on manuscripts and in personal copies of his books, contradict the dating in *Selected Poems* and suggest that most dates given before 1940 are for note versions of poems only.[17] The hiatus seems undeniable, there being ten years between *Trial of a City* and *Ice Cod Bell or Stone* and in *Selected Poems* only seven poems dated between 1953 and 1957. In a paper delivered in 1954 Birney described himself as "a Sunday poet, sometime novelist, and fitful semi-pro in Canada's radio and television, writing in the guilty moments stolen from a professor's schedule."[18] Birney has been a "Sunday poet" throughout most of his career—a writer for whom writing is always secondary to other activities. It is not surprising that many of these activities leave their mark on his work—that they influence its style and partly define its concerns.

27

II

THE NOVELS

From fall of 1926 when he first had his attention turned
to modern fiction by Pelham Edgar, Birney had thought
of himself as a potential novelist. His early interest in
fiction is evident in the concentration of his first *Canadian Forum* articles on Dos Passos, Dreiser, Farrell, and
Faulkner, and in his first major scholarly publication "Aldous Huxley," in Pelham Edgar's *The Art of the Novel*.
As we have seen, when World War II pushed him into
a belated start on his writing career, he turned only con-
descendingly to poetry: "there were things I wanted to
say and I didn't have time to say them in any lengthier
way." After his war service, he felt that his experience
insisted on definition.

> I was back from four years in the Canadian Army, a
> complex unit of my life completed, forever finished
> with—except in my mind, which demanded that it be
> assessed, and emotionally contained. (*CW*, 39-40)

Apparently even more insistent, as he revealed to Al
Purdy, was his wish to be financially independent:

> That's what I wanted more than anything else . . . to
> make enough money from that [*Turvey*] so that I'd
> never have to teach again. . . .I knew I'd never write

28

anything else as popular as *Turvey*. I didn't want to.
(Interview, February 2-9, 1968)

Armed with these dual and possibly incompatible motivations, Birney set about writing the first draft of *Turvey* on Bowen Island in the summer of 1948; he managed to revise it for publication during the following academic year.

Turvey, like *Down the Long Table* which followed it in 1955, is a semi-autobiographical novel. The title character is a composite of many of the cheerful undereducated soldiers Birney had interviewed during his career as Personnel Selection Officer. Turvey's misadventures include both Birney's own wartime medical misfortunes and many escapades he had learned of while investigating battalions with severe discipline and morale problems.

> He'd crystallized in my mind out of a number of
> people: a lovable batman I once had; scraps of memories of those hundreds of youths I had interviewed or
> with whom I'd shared the wards of army hospitals.
> And Turvey had emerged also out of myself, out of
> all my own well-intentioned stupid boners as a soldier,
> and my own comedies and near-tragedies and loves
> and hates and fears in the king's uniform.
>
> (CW, 40-41)

Although most of the officers would appear to be caricatures of men the author knew, Birney himself makes an appearance as a PSO who interviews Turvey. Also, Birney's own non-combat role is reflected in the military career of Private Turvey, the reluctant non-combatant who spends most of the war assigned to holding units. The only other character who plays a more than incidental part in the novel is Turvey's companion and idol, Mac (Captain MacGillicuddy), whom Birney inserted into the book strictly on academic grounds after realizing his work's similarity to *Don Quixote*.

> Thinking of Don Quixote, for example, made me realize that *my* hero was a Sancho Panza, and so I must invert Cervantes' form, create a Quixote only as a secondary character, as a romantic, crazy officer Mac, whom Turvey is always trying to find. (*CW*, 41)

Turvey is subtitled "a military picaresque," and is faithful to the picaresque form in being a succession of episodes strung chronologically along the travels of its rogue hero. Like the picaresque also, the novel focuses on the exterior of its characters and dwells on their identifying idiosyncrasies. It is interested in action rather than psychology, in comic stereotype rather than personality. The plot follows Private Thomas (Tops) Turvey's frustrated military career from his enlistment struggle with a psychological test through countless Canadian and European barracks, trains, and hospitals to his discharge in Toronto. Along the way he agitates to be assigned to the near-mythical Kootenay Highlanders regiment, searches for his friend Mac, drinks, gambles, fornicates, and goes AWOL—anything to break the tedium of barracks life. Turvey continually suffers from the incompetence and inefficiency of his superiors. He is needlessly injured on a condemned obstacle course, he is assigned for officer potential evaluation by officers who are using him as a decoy in order to retain better soldiers, he is termed psychotic by an ambitious personnel officer who is trying to impress his superiors, he is nearly killed by medical personnel who are ignorant of the after-effects of diphtheria. Toward the end of the novel Mac is killed in a rare mortar barrage; his death is curiously given much less emphasis than many of Turvey's debauches. Then, for an unexciting hundred pages, Turvey lies in a hospital bed with diphtheria and woos and wins his true love.

For a war novel by an ex-Marxist, *Turvey* is a remarkably good-humoured book. It has been called by George Woodcock "a gay but angry tract of the times."[1] While it does contain some farce and some anger, it is more tedious than gay and certainly aims its anger at few significant targets. As for its being a tract, the mildness of its ironies, its forgiving attitude toward incompetence, and its complete lack of villains make it at best an ineffectual one. The work is far removed from Birney's Rufus columns where he attacked unreservedly all manufacturers of war materials and all bourgeois democracies. Private Turvey has little opinion of the war except that he thinks he'd enjoy fighting.

They aint enough action, least not the right kind. Why I'd better be a woman, that's what! I got a letter from my sister and she says Tilly Salmonberry, she was just a brat when I left Skookum Falls, she's in London now with the CWAC'S, right in all the bombin and, and things. Nobody bombin us. Nobody to shoot at.
(*T*, 50)

Of working-class background and without a steady job before the war, he nevertheless has no animosity toward the more fortunate.

> He began to feel sorry for all the sergeants and staff-sergeants and sergeant-majors and lieutenants he had met. Come to think of it, few of them ever did seem very happy, except maybe when they were swacked. He tried to remember what the really high officers looked like, but he hadnt seen any of them close up so far. (*T*, 79)

He has the emotions and ideals of a canine. He dislikes whatever blocks the immediate satisfaction of his desires, drifts willingly into any opportunity for sexual and gustatory gratification, and tolerates both disappointment and danger with considerable cheerfulness. After he has been shot at by a deranged comrade, we are told:

> Whether it was the indignity of being shot at, however playfully, by his own side, or whether it was Christmas Eve without a pass, or the frustration of not being allowed to shoot back, or just the milder weather, Turvey wasnt sure; but when, after supper, Ballard again raised the topic of going on the loose Turvey found himself listening with more interest. Ballard this time drew a detailed picture of the charms of his two Buffalo friends, the softness of their beds, the comparative variety and abundance of American food, and the bliss of lying-in till mid-day unattended by corporals, sergeants or their betters. By nine that evening they were both on the Niagara Falls road, their

32

cap-badges gleaming in the auto headlights, their right
arms twisted out from them, thumbs wistfully curved.
(*T*, 54)

What is important is that his dissatisfactions, however
sentimentalized, are invariably petty. If the book were
indeed a tract to suggest that individual needs should
override the organizational imperatives of the armed
forces (as Mr. Woodcock would have us believe), it
would have to turn on much more consequential issues
than Private Turvey's boredom with behind-the-lines life.

Instead of possessing the tone of a tract, *Turvey* has
more the light-heartedness of a Broadway play, and it is
not surprising that two musical-comedy versions of the
book have been staged. Incidentally, both have surprised
Birney by their almost pro-war tone. Birney has defended
Turvey's authenticity by pointing to its popularity with
army veterans.[2] What gives it this popularity is un-
doubtedly the extent to which the novel resembles the
tales of war veterans recalling their enlistment adventures.
The novel gives that selective and tolerant view of war
as "not such a bad time really" so peculiar to legionnaires
and so dangerous to civilized life.

Birney tells us that he based *Turvey* on a re-reading
of both Voltaire's *Candide* and Hasek's *The Good Soldier
Schweik* (*CW*, 42); and Mr. Woodcock stresses how
Turvey parallels the struggles in these two books of
"human individuality" versus "inhuman collectivity."[3]
But the differences are more apparent than the parallels.
In *Turvey* the battle lines between individuality and collectivity are not firmly drawn, so that the novelist never
appears to cast blame. The "inhuman collectivity" in

33

Turvey is portrayed as thoughtless and ineffectual, not as willfully malevolent. Further, Birney finds no irony in his hero's idealistic desire to serve a callous state—unlike Hasek and unlike also Georghiu in *The 25th Hour* or Swift in *Gulliver's Travels*, Book II. Birney does less than pull punches in *Turvey*; he fails to enter the ring.

Turvey suffers not only in comparison with the above but with most serious war novels. A comparison with Heller's *Catch 22* is particularly revealing. Ex-Marxist Birney gives us a brief black-market coal incident; Heller in Milo Minderbinder, who will bomb his own outfit if offered sufficient payment, offers a grotesque satire of capitalism. Birney provides accidents which invariably have but humorous or temporary consequences—like Turvey's scorching his genitals with potassium permanganate. Heller's accidents result in macabre scenes such as the severed legs of Kid Sampson quivering upright on a diving raft. Birney's examples of military incompetence, such as the obstacle course incident, have for the most part only minor and tolerable consequences—sprained joints and fractured bones; Heller's send planeloads of men plummeting to death. While the scenes of destruction in Birney's novel are vivid enough—London, Nijmegen, rural Holland—the process of war itself is only amusing, boring, or silly. War is deadly only in the last few pages when the maimed are delivered by their hospital train to their private and crippled worlds.

Brockville, and the strapping CSM from the Tank-Transporter Unit is given a little slip of paper telling him he can go straight home for a month's leave and that his wife and children are waiting at the platform. And he smiles and cocks his wedge-cap over the little plate in his skull and walks out with two punctured ear-drums from the silent car into the silent world.

(*T*, 278)

What prevents *Turvey* from being just another banal and escapist collection of war-jinks is the quality of briefly sustained passages within it. While Birney neither here nor in *Down the Long Table* is able to create a novel which makes a clear and believable statement, he nevertheless can write small constituent passages with the precision and vigour of poetry. Birney's vision of war may be blurred by the cheery glow of Allied victory to the extent that he can seldom see what fuels this glow, but his power to give occasional set-piece descriptions, dialect monologues, and comic conversations is unmarred. It is the lyric poet's craft that is evident in these. The parallels between the opening of chapter seventeen and Birney's poem "Road to Nijmegen" are well known. Another passage about Turvey's return to Canada is vaguely reminiscent of Birney's cross-Canada poems, particularly "North Star West."

Canada, still only half-real, familiar, and yet, because so unchanged, curiously foreign and a little frightening. The endless flow again of evergreens, log-flecked lakes, violently rushing rivers and little wooden stations knotted with people in strange variegated clothes, civilians looking bored, even a little resentful, or filled with a childish noisiness. Then it was night and Turvey's car was its own remote world, a sway-

ing dimlit cylinder of snores and sleepless tossings, of
persistent hopes and fears and, twice in the long night,
of dreams which broke into choked yells from the
twenty-year-old Flight Sergeant tumbling once more
through the flak over Berlin. Morning brought the
Laurentians and the train rushing with full right-of-
way through valleys and villages, stopping only to re-
lease some of its damaged cargo to a tense group on a
platform, and crawling at dusk across the grey St.
Lawrence into the dingy excitement of Montreal.

(T, 277)

Other passages foreshadow the sure handling of mono-
logue that marks poems of the fifties and sixties such as
"Billboards Build Freedom of Choice" and "Sinaloa." As
George Woodcock has noted, nearly every Canadian
speech pattern is represented in Turvey; in addition
several fascinating characters are portrayed by dialogue
alone. One of them is Sergeant Sawyer, "the merriest
short-arm inspector in the Canadian Army."

> "Allri unbuttonyahtrousehs . . . allawaydown . . .
> evradadose? . . . lesseeit . . . Okaynexman . . .
> chokeit . . . HARD . . . cmon, can' hurta lil feller . . .
> nexman, opnup . . . jeeze, Niagara girls'll be glada
> thisn . . . Okaynexman . . . any RC's here? . . . report
> ta padre right af'er this prade . . . cmoncmon nexman,
> get em comin faster corpral . . . allri dont be shamed
> it plup your shirt. . . ." (T, 45)

Another is Clarence, the ingenuous and adenoidal
orderly.

"I miscodducted byself. With a Digglish girl. Dad-cy's her dabe. O, she's really a very dice girl though. She was assistig a kebbist, they call eb. Kide a like a drug store. Id Habberspith. But thed of course she got fired." He stopped and heaved again. "Wish I'd brought adother bottle." (*T*, 250-251)

When writing *Turvey* Birney may have thought of himself as a delayed novelist who had finally abandoned his time-saving "novelist's poems" and turned to his true calling, but the evidence in the novel suggests quite the opposite. The novel is poorly conceived and structured; it makes a much less important statement about the war than does Birney's prose poem "Joe Harris." But particularly in its dialogue *Turvey* points the way to the more natural form and diction which characterize Birney's poems of the fifties and sixties—poems important enough to re-establish his literary stature late in his career. For while Birney's first books of poems are written in the controlled literary diction and syntax established by the Auden school in the thirties, *Turvey* is written largely in North American speech idioms. And it is only when Birney brings these idioms to his poetry that his full potential as a poet becomes apparent. However, immediately after *Turvey* Birney did not return his full attention to the publishing of lyric poetry. His next two large works are the poetic drama *Trial of a City* (1952) and the novel *Down the Long Table* (1955). The drama, to be examined in chapter three, is an even greater excursion into North American speech patterns than is *Turvey* and, like the novel, it represents another important step in

Birney's development from a British-oriented to a North American-oriented poet.

Whereas *Turvey* is Birney's attempt at a commercially successful novel, *Down the Long Table* is his single attempt at a major piece of fiction. It is an overwhelmingly serious work, somewhat complicated by a variety of borrowed technical innovations, and devoted to the analysis of character rather than the exploration of comic foibles. While *Turvey* offers the surface of a limited man's adventures, *Down the Long Table* attempts to penetrate the depths of a complex and self-doubting academic mind, that of Gordon Saunders, graduate student in Chaucerian studies and sometime Marxist in Canada of the 1930s. As in *Turvey*, large sections of this novel are autobiographical, but unlike *Turvey*, the character of the protagonist is almost entirely so. Thus the second novel is more ambitious than the first not only from a literary viewpoint but also from a psychological one. For in appraising and justifying Gordon Saunders' life Birney is in effect explaining a portion of his own. In this sense, his understanding of Saunders can never surpass his understanding of himself.

The central action of *Down the Long Table* occurs within a brief narrative frame—a hearing held by a U.S. congressional committee, some time in the early 1950s, to investigate the political backgrounds of influential academics. Brought before this committee and questioned aggressively about his affiliations during the thirties, Gordon Saunders silently recalls the confused activities of the person he once was. His recollections begin in 1932 when he was a fledgling instructor at a small Mormon college in Utah, and conclude seven years later with him married and an established Chaucerian scholar at a "fabulous" American university. The book is, therefore, a coming-of-age novel, following its hero through youthful vacillations and self-deceit to his self-dramatizing grandiloquence of the concluding page. Substitution of the University of Utah for the small Mormon college and the University of British Columbia for the American university provides the rough outlines of the parallel period in Birney's life. The novel's major difficulty is that the hero never really comes of age. In the opening chapters we see him as the ineffectual and naïve lover of a married woman, his paralyzing indecisiveness leading indirectly to her death at the hands of an abortionist. In the centre of the book we see him overwhelmed by Thelma, a beautiful, illiterate, and immature Trotskyist. Toward the end his naïveté is chiefly political, as he makes a series of painfully ineffectual attempts to organize a Trotskyist cell in Vancouver.

Throughout the book Gordon is dominated by the people around him. Anne, the married woman, alternately indulges and scorns him as if he were a young boy. The Toronto Marxists keep him continually in the role of the humble student. Thelma manipulates him to various selfish and political ends. The Vancouver Marxists think of him as "a summer rebel." And his relationship with his one true friend in the novel, Professor Channing, never matures beyond that of teacher-student. Yet on the last page of the book, as Saunders is returning his attention to the 1950s and to the congressional committee which he is facing, Birney asks the reader to believe that his hero has indeed come of age, and will at last begin to confront those who seek to repress or humiliate him.

And Gordon Saunders, *alias* Paul Green, who had not made his history either but had lived it, began now to speak it out, neither in fear nor guilt nor pride, but because it was himself and he was a man alive, staring down the long table. (*DLT*, 298)

But he offers only rhetoric to support this request—no facts, no actions. Saunders may well be deceiving himself once more and be destined to continuing ineffectuality.

In a sense it is this last page, with its dubious vision, which is the only important flaw in the novel's conception. If the work were merely the story of a sensitive and ineffectual man, that is, if it lacked the frame provided by the McCarthy-style investigation into which the bulk of the novel is set, it would be greatly improved. But Birney apparently could not retire to such distance from his central character. He had to insist on this character's ultimate strength, and so in a way reduce the book to an unconvincing *apologia pro vita sua*. In his attempt to rationalize Saunders' life Birney leaves even the question of whether Saunders has sold out in deserting Marxism unsatisfactorily answered. Professor Channing urges Saunders not to assume responsibility for the death of an informer the police had placed within the Trotskyists and thus jeopardize his academic career. In response Saunders not only follows this advice but inexplicably says goodbye to the entire Marxist movement. Has he sold out? Certainly a man as idealistic as Saunders appeared during his attempts to join the Marxists would not have left without considerable hesitation and reflection, but in the novel he gives the situation neither. Again it seems likely that the real Earle Birney of the thirties has interfered with the work, that an ambivalence in Birney about his own desertion of Marxism at the beginning of World War II has prevented him from drawing a clear portrait of his double.

From a technical viewpoint *Down the Long Table* is more uneven than *Turvey*. The effect of many brilliant passages is marred by a few pages of overwriting at the beginning and end and by an overdependence on derivative techniques. The most obvious of the latter is the Dos Passos-inspired social collage in which Birney juxtaposes newspaper headlines, social notes, popular poems, snippets of news items into single chapters in order to establish the social background of the novel's events. While the technique works, and while Birney himself used it as early as 1936 in the Rufus column, the lack of originality is nevertheless disturbing.

Yet *Down the Long Table* is better organized and sustained than *Turvey*. Further, its scenes have a greater vividness than many of those of the earlier novel, being written for verisimilitude rather than for humour. Like *Turvey, Down the Long Table* foreshadows Birney's later poetry. It contains a similar number of character portrayals through dialogue alone; particularily memorable are those of the drunken Saunders in Utah, of the young Marxist intellectuals in Toronto, and of the radical unemployed in Vancouver.

"Maybe you is better Marxist as me," Hansen retorted in his lilting serene way. "But I yoost sayin what that fallah Paul Laforgue say. Right to be Lacey. Book you fallahs wass sellin, by French comrade was side-

41

kick of Karl Marx. He talkin about real Vurkers State tew, when everybody got time to enjoy life, money tew, workin big wages maybe ten hours a veek and den have right to be lacey any vay he can, sailin yachts mebbe even, in English Bay, not yoost sit on his ass on grass like ve is doin." (*DLT*, 218)

It also contains several set-piece stylistic exercises that are again notable for their similarity to Birney's poems of the sixties. Gordon Saunders' parable of the bathers (*DLT*, 70-76) is a skillful exposé of his blurred romanticism. And the letters from Van Bome (*DLT*, 96-98) and from Thelma are particularly strong, the latter being a devastating revelation of all that the reader has suspected of her character.

> . . . that dummy and Willie are living together, everybody says so and I think that's terrible we should leave that kind of morals to the Stalinites. And anyway it makes him predjudiced. Of course Leo spoke up for me, and Ronnie and Hymie naturally they said some really sweet things the smoothies, you'd have been pleased, I hope but Willie's gang all raved about Rosie. Leo says Willie has a secret faction right in our group that's tied up with the Fieldites in New York of all things, that bunch of bohemeans, and Field is really Bauerite, you know that ultraleftist they expelled in Paris and Trotsky had to write a pollemic against because they kept bringing up a lot of hair splitting points about theory though all they really want is to get the leadership away from the Old Man and set up a 4th Interntl rite away, isnt that terrible?
> (*DLT*, 229)

In general, *Down the Long Table* would seem to be not only the better of the two novels but also the more interesting from a writer's viewpoint. *Turvey*, a novel of extended plot, caricature and attempted comedy, has neither the obvious strengths nor flaws of *Down the Long Table*, a novel of character. While the mediocre *Turvey* is written for humorous effect, *Down the Long Table* seems written as a search for the truth about a man, perhaps a more hazardous task. Thus *Turvey* is praised by legionnaires for its accuracy to army life, and *Down the Long Table* criticised by Desmond Pacey for failing "to bring back the peculiar flavour of the hungry but hopeful thirties."[4] Pacey seems to have missed the fact that in *Down the Long Table* the character of the protagonist is more important to Birney than is social documentary. As a novel of character, *Down the Long Table* also escapes another of Pacey's criticisms, that "quotations from Eliot, Auden, Spender, and Day Lewis, result in an effect of bookishness and priggishness."[5] These quotations are a part of Saunders' mental life; he is often a bookish prig. So far the virtues of *Down the Long Table* have gone publicly unrecognized. The work was largely ignored by reviewers on publication and has received little attention since. Birney's own immediate reaction was to return to scholarship, and in a few years to move back to poetry. In *The Creative Writer* (1966) he speaks of being "nagged by a third novel" (*CW*, 44), but to this date he appears to have resisted its call.

III

THE LYRICS

Birney's first two books of poetry, *David and Other Poems* (1942) and *Now Is Time* (1945), both received Governor-General's awards, and made the new poet almost instantly a part of his country's literary establishment. "David," the title poem of the first volume, despite fourteen previous rejections, received such praise that for the next twenty years Birney was disparaged for never again having equalled his initial achievement. Until 1962 and the publication of *Ice Cod Bell or Stone* Birney presented the strange case of a poet who began at the apparent height of his powers and who revealed in subsequent poems an unspectacular decline.

The quality of most of the poems in *David* is unquestionable, yet it is also certain that part of the book's favourable reception was due to its timeliness. Birney's immersion in political events throughout the thirties is evident in both the concerns of the book and the way it captures the mood of a nation going reluctantly to war. The best poems are the ones which approach this mood obliquely: "David" (*DOP*, 1-11), an initiation to experience and death, "Hands" (*DOP*, 28-29), a reverie on how nature's violence contrasts with man's, "Vancouver Lights" (*DOP*, 36-37), a reverie triggered by the chang-

44

ing lights of Birney's native city. The worst are direct statements: "Eagle Island" (*DOP*, 23-25), a repudiation of civilization and Ontario, "On Going to the Wars" (*DOP*, 38-40), a laboured, overstated exploration of the author's enlistment. Throughout the volume, whether the poems are directly about war or merely about the changing of the seasons, the images are predominantly violent and the metaphors and analogies frequently military. Many of these have been studiously observed and listed by Desmond Pacey.[1]

Although the "loping" rhythms of "David" have occasionally been referred to as indigenously Canadian, the form of many of the lyrics in Birney's first book reveals in him an orientation that is both traditional and somewhat British. Most of the poems are written inside formal patterns: modified Anglo-Saxon, modified sonnet, couplets, triplets, anapestic pentameter, blank verse. Throughout the poems there is a considerable interest in external finish, often at the expense of the overall effect. As in much of Birney's work, there is an overfondness for adjectivals—adjectives and similes in particular—which indicates a tendency to strain for poetic effect. The strain is most apparent in the rhetorical "On Going to the Wars" where many of the lines mar the poem by their forced cleverness. Even a poem such as "Hands" shows a remarkable dependence on adjectives, a dependence that often increased in Birney's later books.

Back to the safe dead
Wood of the docks, the whining poles of the city,
And to hands the extension of tools, of the militant
typewriter,

45

The self-filling patriot pen, back to the paws
Clasping warmly over the bomber contract,
Applauding the succulent orators, back to the wrinkled
Index weaving the virtuous sock, pointing the witch
    hunt,
While the splayed fist thrusts at the heart hereafter.
                                        (*DOP*, 28-29)

Birney's stance in many of the poems is reminiscent of
that of British poets of the thirties. He frequently takes
the role of the poet as authority ("Monody on a Century,"
DOP, 27), poet as spokesman for that nebulous "we"
("European Nocturne," *DOP*, 35, October in Utah,"
DOP, 19) or poet as omniscient observer ("Anglosaxon
Street," *DOP*, 14, "In this Verandah," *DOP*, 34).

We hunchbacks wheel to the lanes
flashing the whites of our jaws
gophering into the fresh tombs
for a ruby and grandiose apotheosis.
                        ("European Nocturne," *DOP*, 35)

To be sure, many of the best poems in *David* are solidly
based on directly testified personal experience ("Vancouver Lights," "Hands," "Dusk on English Bay," *DOP*,
30-31, "Grey-Rocks," *DOP*, 20); yet it is the presump-
tive stance that will engage Birney most frequently in
his next two volumes.

In his next book, *Now Is Time*, Birney sets out deliberately to chronicle his period and his contemporaries. The
somewhat accidental topicality of *David* becomes enforced in *Now Is Time* by the placing of poems in such

subsections as "Canada, 1937-1942," and "Europe, 1942-1945." Clearly Birney is attempting to take some sort of overview of his world and set himself up as an authority about it. The initial stanzas of the book are openly professorial, and set the tone for what follows:

> Now every spraying syllable
>   veneering private gain
> Shall gloss another farmboy for
>   the toy-display of pain.
>
> For ten lies from a radio
>   and twenty on a page
> a hundred thousand charming eyes
>   will aim the atom's rage. ("Status Quo," *NIT*, 3)

A poem such as "Death of a War" contains all the elements of this professorial and authoritarian pose: the assertive statements, the presumptuous "our," the claim to omniscient vision.

> The fire of the people falls
> but over prairie and peak the grime
> of our living wreathes and appalls;
> the reeking smoke of our times
> clouds every peering eye, and the children's fists
> are smutted with history. (*NIT*, 53)

Unlike *David* which contained a number of personal and partially personal lyrics, the new poems of *Now Is Time* are largely ones of social statement. They are, with some exceptions, about subjects external to the author rather

47

than testimonies of the author's emotion. Two of the exceptions happen to be the poems most highly regarded today, "Road to Nijmegen" (*NIT*, 42-43) and "Joe Harris" (*NIT*, 23-27). It may be significant that most of the poems in this volume were written in England at a time when Birney was in contact with various English poets—George Barker, Henry Treece, and Margaret Crosland. As in *David*, many of the poems are formally conservative. Again many stray from natural Canadian syntax to achieve a poetic effect through rhetorical syntax and excessive modification; "Poem" (*NIT*, 28), "And the Earth Grow Young Again" (*NIT*, 34-35), and "Lines for a Peace" (essentially an Audenseque prayer) are the obvious examples.

> While shadow-seconds race our sea
> below the milky waves of might
> the mind says yes and yes and Be
> and beautiful the fisted light.
> Let fear like rockweed flail and bind
> our waters' flesh, the schizoid quell
> as roots unhook the pavement's mind
> and grasses husk the pavement's yell.
> Let leaf's unhuman humours crust
> within our over-valiant blood,
> find housing for the migrant Must,
> for blasted Shall. (*NIT*, 5)

The Strait of Anian (1948) was subtitled "Selected Poems" and consisted largely of poems reprinted from the two earlier volumes. Like *Now Is Time*, it is divided into subsections. Entitled "One Society" and "One World," these again indicate both a social concern and a drive to achieve overview. The nineteen new poems reflect an even greater dependence on the professional poet's pose of omniscience. They contain not one personal lyric. All are devoted to subjects external to the poet's self, subjects as extensive as Montreal, the Laurentian Shield, New Brunswick, and the Atlantic and Pacific oceans. For the most part the new poems are laureate addresses to a general audience—presumptuous, professorial, and imperative.

Come then trailing your pattern of gain or solace
and think no more than you must
of the simple unhuman truth of this ocean,
that down deep below the lowest pulsing of primal cell
tar-black and still
lie the bleak and forever capacious tombs of the sea.
("Atlantic Door," SA, 3)

The liberties the laureate poet takes with the subjects of his poetry are evident throughout Birney's work, but are taken perhaps most frequently in the new poems of this volume. The presumptuous use of the second person plural seems automatic here, and occurs in about one-half the poems. The presumptuous Audenesque imperative is also fairly commonplace, most obvious in "Ulysses" (SA, 79) and "Gulf of Georgia" (SA, 36), but present in at least another three of the new poems.

Behold this great green girl grown sick
with man, sick with the likes of you.
Toes mottled long ago by soak

49

of seaports, ankles rashed with stubble,
papulous with stumps and scarred with stables.

("New Brunswick," SA, 6)

Also continuing is Birney's tendency to impose irrelevant external form on his material. The Anglo-Saxon metres of "Mappemounde" (*SA*, 4) have nowhere the appropriateness of the earlier "Anglosaxon Street." Rhetorical patterns out of Dylan Thomas are borrowed to carry poems such as "Man is a Snow" (*SA*, 80), "Atlantic Door" (*SA*, 3), and "Gulf of Georgia."

Dive from the shining fluted land
   through the water's mesh
to the crab's dark flower and the starfish.

Trail the laggard fins of your flesh
   in the world's lost home
and wash your mind of its landness. (*SA*, 36)

But most striking in the new poems is Birney's complete commitment to the role of the poet as authority. From his country's chronicler in *Now Is Time* he has now become his country's interpreter. The book's first section "One Society," which contains all but five of the new poems, begins and ends with declarative interpretations of the significance of her eastern and western oceans. It contains portraits of Montreal and New Brunswick, godlike overviews of a prairie family and of Toronto life, a confident analysis of the significance of the Ontario taiga, and a "Case History" of Canada. The difference between these poems and the best lyrics of

David is enormous. No longer is Birney relating what he sees ("Slug in Woods," *DOP*, 13, "Anglosaxon Street") or reporting the thoughts that external sights and events have stimulated within him ("Hands," "Dusk on English Bay," "Vancouver Lights"). Instead of presenting phenomena which demand of the reader precise interpretation, he is now presenting interpretation itself. Between the lyrics of *David* and the new lyrics of *The Strait of Anian*, there is a specific change in technique. There is a movement away from the particular and toward the overview, away from presenting personal thought as phenomenon and toward presenting it as fact, a movement away from the indirection of visual art and toward propaganda. The new poems of *The Strait of Anian* seem the poems of a man overly secure in reputation, and too ready to teach. But fortunately Birney's sense of personal infallibility did wane; he eventually reversed most of the tendencies toward interpretive statement visible in those second and third volumes.

Before his next book of poems, *Trial of a City* (1952), came the qualified success of *Turvey* and the certain achievement of its dialogue. *Trial of a City* owes far more to this novel than it owes to any of the previous books of poems. For the first time since *David*, none of Birney's older poems are reprinted. The title piece, a verse play which occupies more than one-half of the book, is an exuberant exercise in verbal wit and various speech patterns and verse forms. It is even more successful than *Turvey* in delineating unidimensional characters through dialogue. The lyrics of *Trial of a City* are stylistically transitional. Some ("Ballad of Mr. Chubb," *TC*, 61-62, "North Star West, *TC*, 53-57) offer a foretaste of Birney's work of the sixties. Yet "Maritime Faces" (*TC*, 49) is authoritarian and rhetorical, "St. Valentine is Past" rigidly formal.

> While he is rooted rock she strikes
> > to foam a loud cascade
> that drowns the jeering gullish wings
> > far crashings in the glade
>
> No more while lizard minutes sleep
> > around a cactus land
> they'll blow their longings out like spores
> > that never grass the sand (*TC*, 70-71)

In most of the poems, Birney continues to take his old omniscient pose, yet it is now less sweeping and the scenes are more consistently specific. Where he seeks overviews, as in "North Star West" and "Page of Gaspé" (*TC*, 52), his use of the airplane allows the view to be actual rather than cerebral. At the same time the pronoun "we" is no longer a general collective but now delineates specific groups and is occasionally merely a substitute for "I." Finally, Birney indulges in much less interpretation of reality than in his previous volume. He is no longer telling the reader what to believe, but, as in "North Star West," is once again reporting experience piercingly and vigorously.

> A forty ton bubble we rise, rise,
> break through clouds like rollers
> burst to a sunlight five miles high
> The professor overbids and goes down three
> His mother orders buttered scones and tea (*TC*, 55-56)

Ten years elapse before his next collection of poems, *Ice Cod Bell or Stone* (1963), ten years during which *Down the Long Table* fails commercially, and Desmond Pacey speculates that Birney may have published his last poems.[2] Pacey's article about him at this time presents him as an overtly "Canadian" writer, setting out to be "the interpreter and chronicler of the Canadian people."[3] Birney's subjects have been Canada's land, her people, and her history. His background has qualified him especially to write of these, for he had experienced both Canada's frontier and her established cities, her mountain wilderness and her universities, the toil of her workers and farmhands and the platitudinous conversations of her wealthy. Among his poems, "David," "Hands," and "North of Superior" have offered both visions of the primeval Canadian landscape and insight into the implications of this landscape for the nation's culture. "Man on a Tractor," "Prairie Counterpoint," "The Ebb Begins from Dream," and "The Damnation of Vancouver" have observed the lives and characters of her citizens, their shrinking humanity and increasing materialism. "Atlantic Door," "Pacific Door," and "North Star West" have revealed Birney attempting to encompass even the size of the country and its meaning to man.

It would, however, require sophistry to claim that Birney's style in these books has been either "Canadian" or individual—as Pacey tries to in terming it "indigenous and independent."[4] Granted, Birney's choice of stanza forms, metres, and points of view has been eclectic, and there is a myth in Canada of an eclectic culture that takes the best from the cultures of Britain, the U.S., and elsewhere without being dominated by any single one. But this myth has not produced a distinctive culture for Canada, and it does not produce a distinctive style for the early poems of Birney. Eclecticism is not properly a style. Another Canadian myth is that the country is characterized by primitive natural forces and rugged terrain. Pacey depends on this in citing Birney's many active verbs of violence and military imagery as evidence of "indigenous style." This myth, of course, has more reality to it; however, since violence and ruggedness are hardly unique to Canada, and not at all dominant properties of her southern cities, they too seem unsuitable choices for the basis of a national style.

At the end of the ten-year hiatus Birney emerges startlingly transfigured as a poet. His attempt to probe and interpret Canada is over. Whether Birney has considered it complete, hopeless, or merely exhausted is impossible to tell. Now Birney's attention becomes overwhelmingly international, taking him not only to Latin America but on two global tours. Ironically, in this period when Canada under Lester Pearson becomes herself an international broker, Birney, by becoming internationally engaged, becomes more "Canadian" than he has been before. An alien among the ubiquitous American tourists, he greets the peoples he visits with a helpless and disinterested sympathy—a response that became characteristic in the sixties of Canada's public attitude to such tragedies as Biafra and Vietnam.

In addition, Birney's style is visibly altered. Almost all the tendencies evident in the lyrics of *Trial of a City* are now fulfilled. Birney's fondness for generalizing has become a fondness for particular people and scenes, even for anecdotes. His fondness for pontificating has become

54

a willingness to discover and be taught. His desire for overview has dissolved into a town-by-town investigation of rural Mexico. Concern with external form has become concern with organic form. The pronoun "I" has completely replaced "we." Rhetoric has for the most part yielded to conversational diction and rhythms; the most memorable poems are no longer Audenesque ones like "Atlantic Door" but dialogue poems—"Mammorial Stunzas for Aimee Simple McFarcin" (*ICBS*, 19), "Sinaloa" —which seem certain progeny of the colloquial *Turvey* and "Damnation of Vancouver."

Hokay, you like bugambilla, ow you say, flower-hung
     cliffs?
Is how old, the Fort? Is Colhuan, muy viejo, before
     Moses, no?
Is for you señor,[5] take em away, send us helevator for
     weat.
It like me to see all them fine boxcar stuff full rice,
sugar, flax, all rollin down to those palmstudded ports
were Cortez and all that crap (you heat history?)—
     and bugger the pink flamingos.
                              ("Sinaloa," *ICBS*, 42)

This is not to say that Birney's transformation is total. "Can. Lit." (*ICBS*, 18) is essentially an abstract statement, and "Twenty-third Flight" (*ICBS*, 33) shows that the poet's love of rhetoric has not died. But even where Birney indulges his desire to manipulate form, as in "Sestina for the Ladies of Tehuanteec"[6] (*ICBS*, 54-55), the formal elements, instead of distracting from the content of the poem, now provide a way for sharper perception of this content.

Birney's shift from public man to private man, from presumption of knowledge to considerable humility, and from treating the poem as an aesthetic object to viewing it as an avenue toward truth continues in *Near False Creek Mouth*. Again the shift is not complete. "November Walk" (*NFCM*, [1-9]) in particular is marred by argumentative similes, an overabundance of adjectives and descriptive passages, and a general heavy-handedness in its moralizings. And yet even this poem is remarkable for its private, intimate tone and its freedom from preconceived structure.

> Something   is it only the wind?
> above a jungle of harbour masts
> is playing paperchase with the persons
> of starlings   They sift and fall
> stall and soar   turning
>
>> as I too turn   with the need to feel
>> once more the yielding of moist sand
>> and thread the rocks back to the seawall
>>> (*NFCM*, [7])

The short lyrics of this volume are generally not as good as those of *Ice Cod Bell or Stone*. The few that return to wit, pontification, and closed form ("Orphiasco," "Can. Hist.," "Fine Arts," "Candidate's Prayer," "Testimony of a Canadian Educational Leader") are clever but limited. There are a number of dialogue poems, one ("Billboards Build Freedom of Choice," *NFCM*, [64-66]) outstanding, but others (particularly "Most of a Dialogue in Cuzco," *NFCM*, [43-48]) severely forced. There are many personal lyrics, most of these unburdened with excessive interpretive intrusions. But quite a few are inconsequential, particularly those where Birney imposes his newly found humility on his sexagenarian sexuality— "Curacao" (*NFCM*, [18]), "On the Beach" (*NFCM*, [19]), and "Saltfish and Akee" (*NFCM*, [16]). This humility is no more convincing a pose than the earlier knowledgeability. The significant lyrics of this book, "Transistor" (*NFCM*, [11-14]), "Meeting of Strangers" (*NFCM*, [20-21]), "Cartagena de Indias" (*NFCM*, [29-34]), "Memory No Servant" (*NFCM*, [35]), "Machu Picchu" (*NFCM*, [53-57]), are direct and unpretentious, and written in the flexible forms and authentic voice which Birney mastered in *Ice Cod Bell or Stone*.

> Stubbornness   when I practise it
> looks to be no more operative on history
> than Boadicea's   The Romans always win

So the lords of the Inca   grilling
in Cuzco on the spit of Pizzarro[7]
rather than say which mountain
hid the Holy City   seemed
for the next four centuries
to be as ineffectual as early Britons
     or late Canadians ("Machu Picchu," *NFCM*, [53])

As a stylist, Birney travels an enormous distance between The Finger and False Creek. Along the route he masters a greater variety of forms than any other Canadian poet so far, and writes poems which are classics of their kind despite wide divergences in style: "David,"

"Anglosaxon Street," "The Road to Nijmegen," "Damnation of Vancouver," "A Walk in Kyoto," "Sinaloa." That he could not leave his early limitations entirely behind may be regrettable, but it does not detract from Birney's great accomplishment in bringing the author of "Atlantic Door" to write "A Walk in Kyoto" or "Meeting of Strangers."

In 1966 Birney gathers together ninety-nine poems from the preceding books and publishes them with one other as *Selected Poems*. All but eight of the ninety-nine he has revised in some way. These revisions deserve more detailed study than space here permits; in general they would seem attempts to modernize—to relieve unnatural syntax, to remove or conceal external form. The most obvious revisions are those of punctuation; almost all conventional marks have been replaced by space within the line or by line breaks. The effect of this change on older poems is to replace an emphasis on literary form with one on speech rhythms, and thereby to present the poem as spoken word rather than as aesthetic object. Thus "Waterton Holiday," which once began

By these leisurely waters wander
the tired dandelions, (*DOP*, 12)

becomes "Holiday in the Foothills," beginning

By these leisurely waters   wander
   the tired   dandelions (*SP*, 115)

Less obvious are the weakening of rhyme schemes and the general elimination of excessive descriptive elements.

By these changes "Smalltown Hotel" becomes "De-composition."

> Cornered by two sprawling streets
> The yellowed stiff hotel is stuck
> A golden tooth within the buck-
> Mouthed prairie town. Agape it greets
> The evening's halfmoon sky.　　Within
> The fly-loud dining-room a thin
> Old waitress chants the bill-of-fare
> To one bored traveller for kitchen-ware.
>> ("Smalltown Hotel," *DOP*, 21)

> A golden tooth within the buck-
> mouthed prairie town the yellow
> stiff hotel is stuck and stuck
> within it like a deadened
> nerve a thin grey wai-
> tress drones the bill-of-fare
> to one pained salesman for enamelware
>> ("De-composition," *SP*, 115)

The omissions in this collection also provide evidence of Birney's altered perspective on the poet's craft. Many of the impersonal, authoritative poems are missing: "Within These Caverned Days," "Death of a War," "VE-Night." Many of the formally mechanical are also gone: "Status Quo," "Monody on a Century," "Eagle Island." *Selected Poems* is the work of a man who has learned a great deal about poetry in his thirty-year career, and has changed his views on the art radically. Through his revisions and omissions here Birney provides both overt self-criticism of his early work and a clear statement of the poetics of his maturity. Nevertheless, although *Selected Poems* does sum up and confirm a stylistic change that has been occurring in Birney's work over many years, it must be noted that the structures and methods of most of the reprinted early poems are not greatly altered. While a conversational and personal tone does dominate the book and pervade even many of the early poems, *Selected Poems* is still an anomalous volume which documents, despite all revisions, the full range of Birney's poetic interests and accomplishments to 1966. And throughout, no matter how extensive the revisions, Birney carefully dates the poems according to original years of composition—as if acknowledging the impossibility of metamorphosing the attitudes and preconceptions of his youth by stylistic change alone.

Birney's latest book at this writing is *Rag and Bone Shop* (1971). It will not be his last; he has already in manuscript for 1972 publication another gathering tentatively entitled "The Twenty-First Century Belongs to the Moon." *Rag and Bone Shop*'s title is taken from Yeats' "The Circus Animals' Desertion," a late poem in which the Irish poet notes that the romanticism and idealism of his early and middle work have vanished, that there remains to him only the mundane reality from which all dreams spring:

A mound of refuse or the sweepings of a street,
Old kettles, old bottles, and a broken can,
Old iron, old bones, old rags, that raving slut
Who keeps the till. Now that my ladder's gone,

I must lie down where all the ladders start,
In the foul rag-and-bone shop of the heart.

By *Rag and Bone Shop* most of Birney's "ladders" are gone from his poetry also: his Marxism, his notion of himself as a social reformer, his laureate pose of omniscience, his attempt to interpret and romanticize his country. This book is generally in a much lower key than his previous work. It is characterized by detachment and humour rather than involvement and anxiety. With five or six forgivable though maudlin exceptions, it is the book of a wise old man who has extricated himself from man's petty struggles to discover that life is, and has been, simultaneously hopeless, amusing, tragic, and precious. Stylistically this change is reflected in an even further movement from formal structures and academic syntax and diction:

It seems he had a girl in London who sent him Little
    Mags
He planned to join her but was still in debt to shrinks
after a breakdown when he was flunked out from the U
flunked by one of the 3 tame canaries in the English
    Dept.
They ole think Oim bonkers   he whispered over
    the bar table
(as if we were really Underground)

("Kiwis," *RBS*, [52]).

It is also reflected in a lowered dependence on adjectivals as Birney's new detachment frees him from the necessity of arguing and justifying awkward interpretive views.

61

Birney's preferred part of speech is now the noun or noun cluster:

> . . . those first compulsive whites   the Searchers
> for gold   absolution   furs   or mere difference
> came hurtling in improbable canoes   heavy with
>   liquor
> and fear   bearing their beads and syphilis
> muzzleloaders and god
>   ("The Mammoth Corridors," *RBS*, [12]).

This shift in dependence from adjectival to nominal parallels the shift in Birney's interest from what could be to what is. The most extreme evidences of this shift are the concrete and semiotic poems, which are here gathered from their former occasional appearances in earlier collections and from the Birney issue of *Gronk* magazine. Some of these ("For Esther," *RBS*, [34], "University," *RBS*, [42], "Up Her Can Nada," *RBS*, [19], "Canada Council," *RBS*, [21]) are nearly pure noun since in syntactic terms they state nothing. They simply exist as visual arrangements of letters and words.

These concrete poems, which grew from typographically assisted poems in *Ice Cod Bell or Stone*, are thus an important part of Birney's evolution in style. The number of them in *Rag and Bone Shop* demands that we take them seriously and consider the issues they raise—the charges of gimmickry Birney assails in his introduction to *Selected Poems* (*SP*, 1x), and the charge of mere cleverness which Robin Skelton levels.[8] Concrete, essentially the employment of linguistic signs for visual effect, is a serious international movement of the 1960s. It flourishes chiefly in Europe and South America but has important practitioners in Canada in B. P. Nichol and Bill Bissett. Concrete is usually divided by its devotees into "clean" and "dirty." In clean concrete, the preferred and dominant type, the visual shape of the work is primary, linguistic signs secondary. In this view the most effective concrete poems are those with an immediate and arresting visual effect which is made more profound by the linguistic elements used in the poem's constituent parts. The weakest are dirty concrete, those with amorphous visual shape and complex and involute arrangement of the linguistic elements. In dirty concrete, there can be no immediate response to the whole, only a cumulative interpretation gained by painstaking labour. In *Rag and Bone Shop*, "Up Her Can Nada" is dirty concrete; "For Esther" clean. Birney, coming to concrete from a linguistic rather than a visual orientation, has created chiefly dirty concrete, poems in which reading is more important than perception of form.

Concrete techniques themselves are certainly legitimate artistic methods. To question them is to question the validity of all visual art. Although they participate only marginally in our culture's dominant system of language transcription (being pictorial and logographic more often than phonetic), they are still methods of such transcription, providing symbol and signal for ideas or objects. In the majority of Birney's concrete work he remains a linguistically oriented poet for whom concrete techniques are auxiliary. In the early pieces ("Mammorial Stunzas for Aimee Simple McFarcin") concrete gives typographical aid to an otherwise syntactically conventional poem. Here its onomatopoetic role is the same as that often taken by alliteration or assonance; its use is no more gimmicky than use of the latter would be. In his later concrete, such as "Campus Theatre Steps" (SP, 34), conventional syntax begins to yield to the semiotic. They are still combined, however, as late as "Alaska Passage" (RBS, [8]) and "Window Seat" (RBS, [45-46]). Even "Like an Eddy" (RBS, [31]) Birney's poem on a mobile, is expressed in a complete sentence. Only in the recent concrete pieces of *Rag and Bone Shop* ("University," "Newfoundland" (RBS, [29]), "For Esther") has Birney's evolution toward detachment, objectivity and noun-dominated language brought him to primarily semiotic techniques.

The stylistic virtues of the best Birney poems of both his early and later periods are a clarity of syntax and a precision of diction. We find these in "El Greco: Espolio":

> The carpenter is intent on the pressure of his hand
> on the awl, the trick of pinpointing his strength
> through the awl to the wood, which is tough.
>
> (*ICBS*, 14)

We find them also in "The Road to Nijmegen":

> At first only the gathering of graves
> along the lank canals, each with a frosted
> billy-tin for motto; the bones of tanks
> beside the stoven bridges; . . . (*NIT*, 42)

In each Birney locates easily le mot juste—"lank" canals, "bones" of tanks, the "pinpointing" of strength—

and with the exactitude of the Jerusalem carpenter. In many poems Birney can rescue a potentially weak passage by suddenly locating such a word; in context the word selection often seems fortuitous and inspired. Such are "sunladders" in "Takkakaw Falls" (*TC*, 64-65) and "whorling" in "Transistor."

> She paused only once   to down a glass
> the engineer poured from the rum he'd brought
> He knew what songs to ask for
> and out they came now whorling
> as if her voice were immortal and separate
> within her   and she only the toughened reed
>
> (*NFCM*, [12])

These felicitous words keep a poem simple and direct; they eliminate the need for excessive modification; most important, they give the appearance of a poet in full command of his medium, and inspire trust in the reader. When Birney fails to locate them he sinks into adjectives and wordiness, as in "Flying Fish."

> From the basalt waves we flake
> bronzed and blue as dragonflies,
> flash into the alien air,
> toward the dry and blinding sky,
> stall and fall and soar and then
> flicker back into our mirror. (*SA*, 56)

Or, as in "For George Lamming," his loss of grip on language lets him fall to sentimentality.

Always now I move grateful
    to all of you
who let me walk thoughtless
    and unchallenged
in the gardens
    in the castles
        of your skins (*SP*, 52)

But the later Birney seldom has to grope for words so
fruitlessly; usually they come to him quickly, precisely.

white-eyed they spit, wash rockscurf off,
turn without rancour from the guarded gate
                    ("Pachucan Miners," *ICBS*, 47)

Or as vividly as the dying turtle's head rises from the
pavement of a Mexican highway:

The sound   a crushed carton
Looking back;
the untouched head
ancient   stretched   and still
moving ("Memory no Servant," *NFCM*, [35]).

The Humanist

Throughout Earle Birney's poetry one subject and one
theme dominate. The subject is man; the theme is the
hope that someday he will mobilize his powers to save
himself. As Birney grows older this hope weakens and
eventually fails, but his love of man grows continually
stronger.

The early humanism of Birney holds that the ideal world can be approached or gained through human reason. Its general assumptions are similar to those which motivated Plato to write *The Republic*, Sir Thomas More to construct his *Utopia*, or Sir Francis Bacon to compartmentalize science and religion in *The New Atlantis*. They are also, of course, the assumptions which led Pelagius to deny original sin, and Compte to place Humanity on the throne of Supreme Being. But inside these assumptions are two very different schools such a humanism can choose: that of Plato and Bacon where the individual is to find happiness in the success of the group or state to which he subordinates his will, and that of More and Jefferson in which the state is designed to allow maximum self-realization of its citizens. In the first, man's glory lies in his ability to create the institutions which enclose him; in the second it lies in his ability to maintain the fragile and necessarily minimal state superstructure which permits his selfhood. Thus the second is not only the humanism which led Jefferson to oppose the Hamiltonian Federalists but that which led Marx and Lenin to see man as potentially selfless and just and to propose spontaneously maintained communism as a possible social order.

While another Canadian poet, E. J. Pratt, chose the first kind—that which praises institutions and corporations —Earle Birney embraced the second, that which acknowledges the competence of individual man. Birney's involvement with Trotskyism in the 1930s was a direct product of this humanism. Trotsky's quarrel with the Stalinists had centred on the latters' indefinite postponement of Lenin's goal of a worker's state without administrative superstructure and their substitution of "police tactics and bureaucratic centralism."[9] When Birney broke with Trotskyism in 1940, his argument was with the movement's means, not its ends, and with its continual backsliding into support of Stalin's "state capitalism" in international disputes.[10]

In Birney's lyrics there is very little doctrinaire Marxism, but the humanism which brought him to Marxism is dominant and pervasive. In *David and Other Poems* this humanism is expressed simultaneously in admiration for what man can do and in horror at how easily he jeopardizes it. The key poem is "Vancouver Lights," with its powerful expression of the irony of man's ambivalent talents.

> These rays were ours,
> we made and unmade them.   Not the shudder of
>   continents
> doused us, the moon's passion, nor crash of comets.
> In the fathomless heat of our dwarfdom, our dream's
>   combustion,
> we contrived the power, the blast that snuffed us.
> No one slew Prometheus.   Himself he chained
> and consumed his own bright liver.   O stranger,
> Plutonian, descendant, or beast in the stretching night—
> there was light. (*DOP*, 37)

Birney stands by this interpretation of man's predicament throughout most of his career. Man's powers could be infinite; where they are finite they are bound not by the supernatural but by himself—"himself he chained." In *David and Other Poems* human hands that can "suture the bayoneted bowel" also "focus the bombsight" ("Hands," *DOP*, 28-29). Mankind who has "fashioned stars" ("Vancouver Lights") can often stir himself only to pollute a harbour ("West Vancouver Ferry," *DOP*, 16) or to foul nature with inboard motor boats and drunken singing ("Grey-Rocks," *DOP*, 20).

In his next volume, *Now Is Time*, published as the war ended, Birney modifies this view only to the extent of suggesting a stronger possibility of man's success. Again, as in "Death of a War," man is vulnerable, foolish and alone.

> Yet around and around our stereotyped dying
> pirouettes dead the abstracted moon
> and the Pleiades pulse no more to our sighing
> than to the dumb tyrannosaur's doom.

And again man's greatness is potential, not real.

> Still the heart is a metal vibrant
> to love in his lightning searches.
> Within yet trembles our will
> to move as electrons alert to his passage,
> to rise from our dirt and fulfil
> the architect's message. (*NIT*, 54)

But now Birney has glimpses of a new social order, of "a peace, distant maybe as Arcturus, / yet spinning white in the telescope of the Heart" ("For Steve," *NIT*, 32). In "Man on a Tractor," one of Birney's few directly Marxist poems, the speaker muses,

> I'd like to see chalets
> for farmhands, and the boys who are left of the tank
>   troop,
> There's room enough in the mountains for them and
>   for tourists.

And he wishes

>   . . . that the crops from the smoking
>   furrows,
> the ache in his back, the smile of his bride, were lines
> in the map of a reasoned future, of lands without
>   private
> traps, or hidden mortars of class, or flame from the sky,
>   (*NIT*, 10).

By the time he writes the lyrics of *The Strait of Anian* and *Trial of a City* Birney appears to strike a balance in his hope and fear for man. In the paired lyrics "Man is a Snow" ". . . Or a Wind" he attempts to delineate his ambivalence. On the one hand man is a destroyer, fouling both nature's rivers and his own blood, destroying animal life, and constructing "useless windows" (*SA*, 80). On the other, in vague Spender-like terms man may "roar free, unwhirl," go "streaming over the future" (*SA*, 81). But now Birney's poems of hope are almost entirely abstract and vague, and this vagueness, as here in ". . . Or a Wind," testifies against the strength of the hopefulness. Man as destroyer, polluter, or killer Birney can portray with particularity and vigour, as in "Prairie Counterpoint" (*SA*, 17-20), "Montreal" (*SA*, 8-10), or "Images in Place of Logging" (*TC*, 68). But after *Now*

Is Time he can speak only abstractly of man as utopian creator; even the generosity and significance of individual men give him difficulty. In "Driftwood" (*SA*, 34-35) his attempts to praise his friend Einar Neilson lead him quickly to sentimentality. A similar fate befalls a later poem for another friend, "For George Lamming" (*NFCM*, [3]). The lengthy "North Star West (*TC*, 53-57) reveals now in Birney a strong mistrust of the common man and everyday life. At the centre of this poem is a dichotomy between the cleanness, order, and peacefulness of the flying aircraft and the "ferment" of traditional life below. In the plane, technology has created its own Eden, complete with "gardening" stewardess, into which the passengers escape "the flood of our days." The plane lifts them above a world where "headlines open old wounds" and washes the entire landscape "clean by height." Although Birney finds the comfort of the plane at times mildly humorous, there can be no doubt at the poem's end that he prefers even Air Canada's utopian illusions to the reality of the world to which he must return.

> We who have ridden the wings of our people's cunning
> and lived in a star at peace among stars
> return to our ferment of earth with a memory of sky
>
> (*TC*, 57)

From *Trial of a City* onward, Birney's humanism takes a different course. In its political aspects it appears only in his many poems of implied social criticism and even there is often manifest only in a disappointment that man has not created a better world. This path leads Birney eventually

71

to the pessimism of the long poem "November Walk Near False Creek Mouth" (*NFCM*, [1-9]). But, in addition, Birney at this time develops a remarkable joy in individual life, a joy which was hardly visible in the early poems (a notable exception is "Joe Harris," *NIT*, 23-27) and which had its first exuberant full-strength appearance in Mrs. Anyone of the verse-play "Damnation of Vancouver." This development parallels the change in Birney's poetic stance from the generalizing professorial spokesman for society to the isolated sympathetic observer of individuals. In *Ice Cod Bell or Stone* this new love of individuals and particulars is exhibited in numerous poems, among them "The Bear on the Delhi Road," "Captain Cook," "El Greco: Espolio," "A Walk in Kyoto," "Bankok Boy," "Sinaloa," and "Sestina for the Ladies of Tehuanteec." It is a love of bold and spontaneous joy.

a carp . . . rising golden and fighting
thrusting its paper body up from the fist
of a small boy on an empty roof higher
and higher into the endless winds of the world.
("A Walk in Kyoto," *ICBS*, 25)

It is a love of women

whose eyes from fires more stubborn than under
hotsprings
flash out a thousand Mayan years before a Diaz.
("Sestina for the Ladies of Tehuanteec," *ICBS*, 54)

It is also a love of the commonplace, of the life of the carpenter who constructed Christ's cross ("El Greco:

72

Espolio," *ICBS*, 14), of the pleasure taken by Pachucan miners in their tequila and women ("Pachucan Miners," *ICBS*, 47-48). In "Captain Cook" the protagonist never does acquire this love and can live only by the energy of his romantic expectations.

Such poems are less frequent in *Near False Creek Mouth*, and while they still involve love contain much less joy. Here Birney finds no pure exuberance to admire, as he did in "Bankok Boy" (*ICBS*, 28). Now he can love only the continually losing struggle of the oppressed, the helpless, or the dying. But Birney's humanism is still evident in his high regard for those who struggle, for the Inca builders of Machu Picchu who never revealed to their Spanish conquerors the location of their city ("Machu Picchu," *NFCM*, [53-57]), or for the Cuzco priest who agitates for land reform in Peru despite knowing that he will be damned by the government as communist ("Letter to a Cuzco priest," *NFCM*, [49-52]). In the latter poem the terms of Birney's admiration are particularly characteristic of his humanism.

> Father   forgive all men if you must
> but only in despite of god
> and in Man's name
>
> . . . .
>
> Pray to yourself above all for men like me
> that we do not quench
> the man
> in each of us (*NFCM*, [51-52])

At this point in his life it is man Birney worships, man who has aspired, struggled, held to ideals, and found joy. If man were to cease these activities, to Birney he would no longer be man.

Thus we find also in *Ice Cod Bell or Stone* and in *Near False Creek Mouth* a clearly stated aversion to the forces that would suppress life's joy and quench that "man / in each of us." Most frequently this aversion appears as anti-Americanism, or anti-North Americanism. The earliest of these poems is "Ballad of Mr. Chubb" (*TC*, 61-62). The message of most of them, such as "Appeal to a Lady With a Diaper" (*ICBS*, 20-21), "Sinaloa" (*ICBS*, 42), "Most of a Dialogue in Cuzco" (*NFCM*, [43-48]), or "Billboards Build Freedom of Choice" (*NFCM*, [64-66]), is that hucksterism and unthinking acceptance of received ideas stultify humanity by preventing accurate and creative thought. In "Honolulu," hucksterism can present only a superficial and clichéd view of that island.

> . . . any guy dont like Waikiki say we got
> more catamarans surfboats fishspearin palmclimbin
> than all them natives saw in a thousand
> years waitin around for us . . . (*ICBS*, 34)

In "Sinaloa" the native speaker decries visitors who value his country only for its quaintness and care nothing for its economic ills. The most damning of the poems are satirical monologues—"Most of a Dialogue in Cuzco," "Billboards Build Freedom of Choice"—in which the speakers indict themselves through their bigotry, platitudes, illiteracy, and illogicality.

O Gerda I thought the *yamas* were the priests, anyway they live O miles higher than Cuzco though even
this is really too high for an ordinary person except to
visit don't you think? . . . Well Howard says it's over
eleven thousand five hundred metres . . . O maybe he
did say feet   yes feet   anyway human beings
just don't live that high not even in the Rockies so how
could THE Incas have had a CIVILIZATION away up
here . . .

      ("Most of a Dialogue in Cuzco," *NFCM*, [45])

Although the bulk of these speakers and the villains of
the other works are Americans, Birney's animus is not
against Americans per se. Canadians can be equally short-
sighted ("Toronto Board of Trade Goes Abroad," *NFCM*,
[58-59]). Further, what these people have in common is
only incidentally their nationality—Americans, after all,
inevitably loom large in a Canadian poet's consciousness.
The common characteristic is a smugness, a satisfaction
with the static and superficial which paralyzes all en-
deavour and prevents any possibility of a better world. It
is a deliberate ignoring of the "Man" Birney believes
within us, a deliberate self-disqualification from creative
mankind.

In Birney's latest poems (*Rag and Bone Shop*) a new
detachment about both himself and the world modifies his
humanism further into simply a tolerant amusement at
man's foibles and resignation about his doom. Unlike the
uncompromising Latin American satires, the "down
under" satires ("Strine Authors Meet," *RBS*, [54-55],
"Kiwis," *RBS*, [51-52], "Museum of Man," *RBS*, [56],
"Christchurch, N.Z.," *RBS*, [53]) offer no suggestion that

man has any potential for change. In the overtly maudlin "Once High Upon a Hill" (*RBS*, [1-6]), Birney even comes to an amused and self-indulgent understanding of his own youthful limitations. At least six of the poems contain untroubled admissions that man's tenure on this planet will soon end. These latter observations are not new to Birney's poetry but the fact that they are unaccompanied by either regret or exhortation to his fellow man for further effort is indeed new. Typical of the tone of this collection is "Charité, Espérance et Foi: A Tender Tale From Early Ca-nada" (*RBS*, [25-26]). With considerable charm and restraint this poem recounts Champlain's vain attempt to make "Christian ladies" of three Montagnais maidens.

> Little Foi wriggled away & split for the woods
> but Espérance & Charité quickly mastered irregular
>   verbs
> & sewing   developed bosoms   went on to
>   embroidery (*RBS*, [25])

Like all of this collection's satires, the poem has for its subject the comedy of human frailty, and not, as in earlier satires, the necessity of the correction of vice. The two girls learn their prayers and table manners, but lose a chance to visit France when they rebuff a lecherous merchant by politely offering to cut out and eat his heart. As elsewhere in *Rag and Bone Shop*, there are no villains. Champlain is fatherly and in his own eyes generous: "he gave them each a wooden rosary / and sent them back to Quebec." The girls have acted with innocent spontaneity to protect their virtue. Even the "méchant marchand

Marsolet" has done no worse than can be expected of an Anglophile who eats meat "both Fridays and Saturdays." The poems of *Rag and Bone Shop* suggest that by 1971 Birney has resolved the question posed by "Man is a Snow" ". . . Or a Wind." He has decided that man is finite, fallible, and limited in insight, will, and morality. In 1945 this answer would have disturbed him greatly; in 1971 he can find man, despite his circumscribed potential, tolerably amusing. He can even, in "The Mammoth Corridors," dispassionately accept man's demise before some future ice-age, the "mother of ice" descending,

> bringing her love   the rounded silence
> a long hard peace. (*RBS*, [14])

Thirty years before, Birney had dared to hope that man himself could achieve such peace and love.

THE PURSUIT OF MYTH

It has always been easy to view Birney as a social critic. His first two books were memorable for their poems against war; his later books for their poems against political injustice in Central and South America ("Caracas," *NFCM*, [22], "Buenos Aires 1962," *NFCM*, [60], "Letter to a Cuzco Priest," *NFCM*, [49-52]). In between he offered poems on the mediocrity of city life ("Anglosaxon Street," *DOP*, 14-15, "The Ebb Begins from Dream," *SA*, 14-15, "Montreal," *SA*, 8-10), poems on environmental destruction and pollution ("West Vancouver Ferry," *DOP*, 16, "Images in Place of Logging," *TC*, 68, "Leaving Yellowstone," *ICBS*, 35), and poems on social injustice ("Man on a Tractor," *NIT*, 7-10, "For Steve," *NIT*, 29-33, "Late Afternoon in Manzanillo," *ICBS*, 45). Further, in most of his books he has included poems of outright statement on historical or literary subjects ("Canada: Case History," *SA*, 51, "Can Lit.," *ICBS*, 18, "Can. Hist.," *NFCM*, [78-91], "Candidate's Prayer Before Master's Oral," *NFCM*, [81]).

But Birney's social commentary, extensive as it is, is only the surface indication of deeper and more complex currents within his work. To regard this commentary either as one of the major achievements of his poetry or even as intrinsically interesting is to do Birney a serious injustice. Separately these poems appear incidental and random writings of little more durability than the particular issues to which they attend. Collectively they are a body of work in which explicit literal statement tends, even in the late poems, to overwhelm art.

> Pumped up from the immigrant ships
> by the great hose of the American-aid Hiway
> labourers from marginal bogs in Galicia
> lengthen the 9-mile ooze of slums
> (2 walls of packingbox   2 of air
> ½ a scraptin roof)
> from which fountain 89 skyscrapers
> Drowned in the cement foam
> rests the National Pan-
> theon   with the 206 bones of Bolívar
>
> ("Caracas," *NFCM*, [22]

As was evident in the examination of Birney's humanism, he is much more than a social critic. In terms of this humanism, his overt statements on specific social issues are minor by-products of a complex and changing system of belief. They are also by-products of another important facet of the poet: his life-long need for the presence of romance and myth. This need, first recognized by Paul West,[11] has made him impatient with the mundane, unsatisfied with the conventional and close-at-hand, and contemptuous of the status quo.

In both his academic career and his writing Birney is undeniably a romantic. The medieval period in literature is remote, exotic, studded with legend and pageantry, and in fact gives us the primary meaning of the word romance. Birney not only chose it for his professional specialty but allowed aspects of it to touch every book he has written. In the later love poems he takes for himself Chaucer's ironic view of himself as a limited and unworthy lover.

I will follow in a small trot only

   not whirling

      O girl from the seafoam

         have pity
not
   again
        to

     whirl ("On the Beach," *NFCM*, [19])

In *Down the Long Table* Gordon Saunders frequently invokes Chaucerian quotations in order to view himself and others with similar ironic distance—as here where he recalls, while aimlessly wasting a Sunday afternoon, Chaucer's satiric jibe at the Clerk: *"What sholde he studie and make hymselven wood"* (*DLT*, 58). Other invocations of the medieval as a measure of the present abound in Birney's work: in *David* there is "Anglosaxon Street," in *Now Is Time* "War Winters," in *The Strait of Anian* "Mappemounde," in *Trial of a City* the summoning of William Langland, in *Near False Creek Mouth* "Professor of Middle English Confronts Monster," in *Rag and Bone Shop* "Oil Refinery." Often Birney sees similarities between the medieval and the present, as between the fragility of life in Anglo-Saxon England and the perils of modern industrialism:

> Hwaet! he is quick again   that thousand-toothed
>   Queller
> whirls his ghosts in our wheels   unleashes or locks
>   them
> Yea he lives again   in our new graveloot
> breath of that sly snake   stifles and clings
> slides from our long ships   coils round our steadings
> Eala! we are lost   in the spell of his loopings.
>   ("Oil Refinery," *RBS*, [15]

Apparently in personal dilemmas Birney also employs this technique of calling up the medieval in order to understand the contemporary. In one poem even he is amused to find himself responding to a tropical lizard, staring at him from an almond tree, by wondering "what / St. George would have done" ("Professor of Middle English Confronts Monster," *NFCM*, [17]).

80

Birney's politics have been particularly coloured by romanticism—as he conscientiously points out in his self-portrait of Gordon Saunders in *Down the Long Table*. Marxism, with its dream of all men living together equitably and harmoniously, attracted Birney in the thirties with the same power as a romantic call back to theoretical feudalism had attracted thousands of readers to Long Will Langland centuries before. Age may have made Birney more realistic, but the basic romantic hope for social harmony ("Transistor," *NFCM*, [11-14], "For George Lamming," *NFCM*, [15]) and the end of poverty and the exploitation of the weak ("Letter to a Cuzco Priest," *NFCM*, [49-52]) has continued to engage him.

As in Birney's politics, in his poetry we find evidence of the romantic's discontent with the actual, the common-place, or the status quo. In "David" he carefully disguises the actual names of the mountains Bob and David climb: Mt. Aylmer becomes "Mt. Gleam," Gerrard becomes "Sundance," Goat Mountain becomes "The Fortress," and Mt. Edith becomes "the Rampart's arete."[12] In his satires he attacks anti-semitism, tourists, modern warfare, the quality of North American life, the industrialization of North America, the lack of industrialization in Central America ("Sinaloa," *ICBS*, 42), youth on the Canadian prairies ("Prairie Counterpoint," *SA*, 17-20), censorship ("Monarch of the Id," *TC*, 58-59), and many other phenomena. At the beginning of his career he was content to write about commonplace Canada—"Kootenay Still Life," "Waterton Holiday." But after *Trial of a City* he set out deliberately in search of exotic subjects. *Ice Cod Bell or Stone* is based both on a global tour which touches such romantic places as New Delhi, The Hellespont, Ellesmereland, Kyoto, Bankok, Wake Island, and Honolulu, and on an extended visit to rural Mexico which gives another litany of exotic place-names: Sonora, Sinaloa, Njarit, Ajijic, Manzanillo, Irapuato, Pachucan, Actopan, Tepoztlan, San Juan de Ulua, Tehuanteec. *Near False Creek Mouth* is only once near the mouth of False Creek in Vancouver, British Columbia. Here too Birney responds to the lure of fascinating places: Curacao, Barranquillo, Caracas, Cartagena de Indias, Guadelupe, Poza Rica, Cuzco, Machu Picchu, Buenos Aires, Santiago de Chile, Nueve Ixtapan, Port-of-Spain, Epidaurus, Madrid.

Birney's preference for the romantic has a considerable effect on his style. First of all, he frequently seeks techniques by which the present can be invested with the past. This is a method similar to Gordon Saunders' instinctive invocation of literary quotations whenever attempting to interpret himself or others. Birney adapts Anglo-Saxon stanza forms in "Anglosaxon Street" in order to create an ironic contrast between past and present.

Ho! with climbing sun, heading from cocoons,
go bleached beldames, garnished in
  bargainbasements,
festooned with shoppingbags, farded, flatarched,
bigthewed Saxonwives, stepping over buttrivers,
waddling back to suckle smallfry, wienerladen.
               (DOP, 14)

In "War Winter" (*DOP*, 33) and "Mappemounde" (*SA*, 4) he uses these forms in questionably successful attempts to bring Anglo-Saxon stoicism to the hardships of World War II. Here, in "War Winter," he addresses the sun:

Not chiefly the month   moulds you, heartcharmer,
to scant hammerdent   on hardiron sky,
not alone the latitude   to lodgers on this
your slantwhirling lackey,   lifecrusted satellite,
this your one wrynecked,   woedealing world.

In poems like "Ulysses" (*SA*, 79) or "In this Verandah" (*DOP*, 34) he extends metaphor toward analogy in order to impose classical mythology on present events; the latter poem shows the three Fates determining the course of World War II:

Now at thread's end the mottled finger
weaves for the arching airboy.
Lachesis fumbles the skein, arthritic.
Beyond the awnings beyond
the shrinking waters the blind
beldame snips with the chromium shears
and you and I and the burnished amateurs
    at Cawnpore and Singapore
    Inkerman and Rotterdam
    Mafeking and Chungking
    and Marathon I and II
    (and III?)
are ravelled in the wool.

In "St. Valentine is Past" (*TC*, 70-71) his return to myth is so complete that it obscures whatever statement the poem was intended to make. In other poems Birney's juxtaposition of present and past history, mythology, or literature is more conventional, taking the form of the concise single-word allusion common to Western literature in this century. Jehova finds his way into "Flying Fish" (*SA*, 56), Joshua into the final lines of "Dusk on English Bay" (*DOP*, 30-31), Phoebus and Prometheus into "Vancouver Lights" (DOP, 36-37), Aztec virgins into the Mexican poems.

Birney can be said to have a fixed habit of contrasting past and present: the Mayan civilization versus tourist Tehuanteec ("Sestina for the Ladies of Tehuanteec," *ICBS*, 54-55), Bolivar's idealism versus Caraca's squallor ("Caracas," *NFCM*, [9]),Incan glory versus Peruvian peasant poverty ("Machu Picchu," *NFCM*, [22]), Hero and Leander versus himself ("Tavern on the Hellespont," *ICBS*, 16), Beowulf, King Arthur, and the Green Knight versus the Canadian wilderness ("North of Superior," *SP*, 112-113). Even "November Walk Near False Creek Mouth" (*NFCM*, [1-10]), in many ways the most technically avante-garde of Birney's poems, contains this kind of contrast—for instance an Eliotic association of tourists and the Magi:

They dangle plastic totems   a kewpie
a Hong Kong puzzle for somebody's child
who waits to be worshipped
back on the prairie farm (*NFCM*, [3]).

Frequently this technique leads him into ill-advised dichotomies between past and present, so that he sees Aztec Mexico as superior to present-day Mexico ("Conducted Ritual: San Juan De Ulua," *ICBS*, 53), Mayan civilization superior to contemporary Tehuanteec (*ICBS*, 54-55), Incan civilization superior to contemporary Peru ("Machu Picchu," *NFCM*, [53-57]) or Anglo-

84

Saxon England superior to 1940's Toronto ("Anglosaxon Street," *DOP*, 14-15). This oversimplification occurs also in two of his long poems, "The Damnation of Vancouver" and "November Walk."

The second important technical result of Birney's romanticism is his constant use of personification in his treatment of nature. Despite his reputation for "expressing much of the essence of the Canadian land"[13] he habitually does not present nature naturalistically. In the poem "North of Superior" (*SP*, 112-113), he asserts that Canada's landscape is devoid of myth and uninformed by legend, religion, history, or literature.

The swordless rock   the heavenless air   and land
that sweeps unwept into an icy main
where but the waters wap and the waves wane

This poem is probably true to Birney's intellectual sense of the Canadian landscape—that to date it bears no overstructure. But emotionally he perceives the landscape much differently. From his first book onward he presents it as vigorously animate and willful. In "David" he sees the mountains as clearly anthropomorphic, with "sprawling shoulders," a peak "upthrust like a fist." A glacier has "a cold breath," a marten moving like quick-silver "scouts" the two climbers; at the end is the lethal "Finger / beckoning bleakly the wide indifferent sky." Elsewhere in the poem the impression of an active animate natural world is supported by Birney's giving to this world vivid and decisive verbs: water "knifed down a fern-hidden cliff," the prairie "glittered," the skyline "pulsed with surging bloom." A great part of the power of "David" is due to the independence and personality Birney manages to attribute to nature in this way.

Other examples of anthropomorphic nature in Birney are commonplace. Representative of these is "Holiday in the Foothills":

By these leisurely waters   wander
     the tired   dandelions
the purple vetch straggle   to the shore
absentmindedly skirting   the cowpads
At the outlet marshes   even the tigerlilies
doze   and the poplars bare their spavined knees
like a senile chorus stilled in midkick
Haphazardly the mountains   are weathering
out of hearing   in the sun (SP, 115).

What is often characteristic of Birney's personification of nature is that he gives it the power of intention and consciousness. In "Dusk on English Bay" the sun "rushes down through Asian skies" to widen "his light on limbs unsexed and severed"; a flame "probes the tenement ruins" (DOP, 30-31). In "Vancouver Lights," as well as a "mountain's brutish forehead," there is a "restless lighthouse" (DOP, 36). In "Climbers," despite the "pointless point of the peak," "stentorian icefalls call" (TC, 69). Perhaps the poem in which the intentionality of nature is most obvious is "Bushed," although here this intentionality is qualified by the poet's making clear that it exists primarily in the mind of its subject.

But the moon carved unknown totems
out of the lakeshore

86

owls in the beardusky woods derided him
moosehorned cedars circled his swamps and tossed
   their antlers up to the stars
Then he knew   though the mountain slept   the
     winds
were shaping its peak to an arrowhead
poised

And now he could only
bar himself in and wait
for the great flint to come singing into his heart

                                  (*SP*, 117)

It would seem, however, that Birney himself is often
"bushed," that like this man of whom he writes, he sees
nature not only as impartial and inexorable but as animate and willful. Birney's love of myth and story would
seem to triumph over his Marxist scepticism and lead
him to fabricate his own myth with which to invest our
"heavenless air."

Birney's poetry is an intermittent search for myth or,
as he expresses it in "The Bear on the Delhi Road," an
intermittent attempt "to free / myth from reality"
(*ICBS*, 11). In his first book he takes a Canadian wilderness that he must intellectually believe unhaunted and
impersonal and transforms it in "David" by imprecision
and personification into a world as mysterious, haunted,
and spiritual as that of *Sir Gawain and the Green Knight*.
And through this setting, a simplified plot, and an ideal-
ization of character, he makes a story of an ordinary
mountaineering accident approach myth. After the essentially chronicling *Now Is Time* and *The Strait of Anian*,

comes *Trial of a City* which contains both a full-scale exploration of the mythology of Vancouver's past and the pageant of provinces of "North Star West" in which the poet and his fellow passengers

> . . . for a space . . . held in our morning's hand
> the welling and wilderness of Canada, the fling of a
>   nation (*TC*, 57).

Having seen his own country come alive, he pursues the stronger myths of the Mayan, the Aztec, the Incan, and the Spanish Catholic in Central and South America. His envy of these myths and cultures is clear in "Guadelupe":

> Ah señoritas
>
> . . . .
>
> it's not till you park
> your Alfa Romeos[14]
> a quartermile from the shrine and
> coifed in black lace from Aragon
> crawl on your silken penitential knees
> over the cobbles
> that I see you have Mexican blood
> running with sins and anesthesias
> richer than any my veins will ever carry
>
>   (*NFCM*, [38]).

The lonely child alone in the Alberta bush with his fantasies and his Henty novels, who later becomes the young man who is overwhelmed by both the beauties of medieval story and the noble hopes of Lenin, seems to find in

Latin America a world which fully supports his imagination. In both "David" and the Latin American poems, Birney appears to be attempting to recreate images he had first encountered in his childhood reading and his medieval studies. In the Latin American ones he finally succeeds. In such a view of his work the books between *David* and *Ice Cod Bell or Stone* seem false starts, his social criticism seems minor work, and his barrenness in the late fifties most understandable. Even the sentimentality of "Once High Upon a Hill (*RBS*, [1-6]), in which Birney nostalgically recalls how San Francisco's Telegraph Hill once appeared to him as an Arcadia, a Matterhorn, a "Roman hideout," a Hopi cliff, and a floating scrap of Genoa, can seem thoroughly in character.

IV

THE MAJOR POEMS

Earle Birney has written a number of poems that approach or exceed one hundred and fifty lines. Not all of them, however, have the complexity and precision necessary to make length indicate importance. Both "Cartagena de Indias" and "Once High Upon a Hill" are weakened by sentimentality. "Machu Picchu," despite its length, is of a single mood and theme. The most significant of Birney's long poems are "David," "The Damnation of Vancouver," "November Walk Near False Creek Mouth," and "The Mammoth Corridors," all of which are not only many-faceted works but also major statements of Birney's changing humanism.

David (1941)

In both structure and subject "David" is the most traditional of Birney's long poems. As a rather sexless elegiac poem of male friendship it is similar in tone to the traditional pastoral elegy. Though it avoids the conventions of the pastoral elegy, it retains a definite overstructure and metrical form, and has thus become for Canadian educators a most acceptable school piece—being anthologized at least twenty-three times. It is written in pentameter quatrains with a fixed *abba* scheme of what Birney terms "assonantal" rhymes. The rhythm is frequently dactylic, which gives it in Pacey's words a "climbing" quality,[1] but the irregular number of unstressed syllables in the line creates frequent iambs and trochees which prevent any tendency toward gallop. Birney tells us that he was guided toward this rhythm and stanza by Archibald McLeish's "Conquistador," and that he decided upon these before beginning to write the poem (Interview, October 26, 1969).

The structure of "David" is almost mechanically definite. The poem is organized into nine sections. David and Bob first see The Finger at the end of part three, and begin to climb it in part seven. Each of the episodes through five and seven is devoted to the scaling of a particular peak. The climax comes appropriately in part eight with the complementary psychological agonies of the two youths on the narrow ledge: David at knowing he is permanently crippled and Bob at David's asking to be pushed to his death below. In part nine a melodramatic and fast-moving section brings the action to a sudden and nostalgic close.

The poem is also structured by several foreshadowing passages. At the end of part three, carefully juxtaposed with the first sighting of The Finger, David and Bob discover the skeleton of a mountain goat.

That day we chanced on the skull and the splayed
    white ribs
Of a mountain goat underneath a cliff-face, caught
On a rock. Around were the silken feathers of hawks.
And that was the first I knew that a goat could slip.

                 (SP, 119)

"Splayed" is the word that Birney uses to describe David's legs five sections later when the youth is similarly impaled on a rock at the foot of a cliff face. Another foreshadowing passage, the episode in which David mercy-kills a broken-winged robin, is juxtaposed with one in which David heedlessly risks his life in order to reach a peak.

>   At an outthrust we balked
> Till David clung with his left to a dint in the scarp,
>
> Lobbed the iceaxe over the rocky lip,
> Slipped from his holds and hung by the quivering pick,
> Twisted his long legs up into space and kicked
> To the crest. Then grinning, he reached with his
>   freckled wrist
>
> And drew me up after. We set a new time for that
>   climb.
> That day returning we found a robin gyrating
> In grass, wing-broken. I caught it to tame but David
> Took and killed it, and said, "Could you teach it to
>   fly?"

(SP, 119-120)

Here is essentially the same argument that David later uses to speed his own death.

> But I curled beside him and whispered, "The bleeding
>   will stop.
>
> You can last." He said only, "Perhaps. . . . For What?
>   A wheelchair, Bob?"

(SP, 122-123)

The setting of "David" is the most developed aspect of the poem. Birney's repeated personification of natural objects makes the rocky wilderness seem alive and purposive. His diction makes every aspect of this world seem vibrant—"the woods were alive with the vaulting of mule deer"; "the flashing and floating round of the peaks"; "a swamp that quivered with frog-song." All through the poem this effect is aided by Birney's uncanny skill at locating the exact word: "quivered with frog-song," "a gurgling world of crystal." After the accident the diction changes, and nature that before seemed energetic and joyful appears "grave-cold," "sun-cankered," "fanged," "spectral," "obscene." As in "Bushed" there is thus a suggestion that whatever joy or evil we see in nature is an attribution by man, in this case by Bob, the poem's narrator. Birney, however, makes no attempt to stress this as the poem's message, and even fails to provide evidence that he himself understands that the two views of nature are, as the poem stands, products of Bob's necessary relativism. With the shift in diction, Birney gives the reader two contrasting rather than contradictory views of nature, neither of which is in any way questioned or limited by the poet. But "David" is in concept a simple poem, perhaps overly simple, and certainly not one in which the poet is eager to grapple with complex problems of philosophy or even characterization.

A further aspect of the setting of "David" is Birney's creation of the impression of gigantic size. At the poem's beginning we are told that "mountains for David were made to see over, / Stairs from the valleys and steps to the sun's retreats." With this openly celestial scale already established as a background for the poem's events, the succeeding images of size are similarly Miltonic. "Pines thrust at the stars."

> The peak was upthrust
> Like a fist in a frozen ocean of rock that swirled
> Into valleys the moon could be rolled in. Remotely
>   unfurling
> Eastward the alien prairie glittered. (SP, 118)

And later David makes "yodels [which] the ramparts redoubled and rolled to the peaks" (SP, 121). Thus with hyperbole and mixed-size figures (a fist in an ocean, a prairie unfurling) Birney sets the stage for larger-than-life people and larger-than-life events. It is a stage for mythic actions set squarely among Birney's "swordless" rocks.

The characterizations in "David" are suitably of the unidimensional kind typically found in myth or romance. Many years after its writing Birney himself noted their shallowness, but attributed it to another cause.

> I think it ["David"] too much on a straight surface level of narrative, that the study of human character is limited in it, limited partly by the form I chose of narrative. When one of the two people . . . is telling the story, it's a little tricky to develop his character very much without mucking up the story. (Interview, February 8, 1968)

"David," however, is a romantic story stressing setting and action, and if changed to give more attention to character, it would be an entirely different poem. As

94

written, the poem gives highly selective, even censored, views of the two youths. We see them interacting only with each other and in the mountaineering context; we hear them speak only twice, at the death of the robin and the death of David. We do not see them at work, at home, nor with women of any age; we are made to pay attention to their youth, their "lengthening coltish muscles," David's "freckled wrist," his exuberant yodeling. Their subjects of conversation seem strangely juvenile and limited, hardly the totality of what would interest youths whose working hours that summer are being spent on a survey crew.

And David taught me

How time on a knife-edge can pass with the guessing
  of fragments
Remembered from poets, the naming of strata beside
  one,
And matching of stories from schooldays. . . .

(SP, 119)

Such a passage makes the two seem mentally schoolboys, and yet they are obviously more. We are also led to see David's expertise at climbing, his knowledge of geology, and his maturity in the face of death. Bob is presented simply as a neophyte, constantly learning from David about both climbing and life. Curiously, the total effect of these sketchy and not entirely harmonious details is to draw two characters of idealized nobility. They result in a David who is graceful, intelligent, selfless, and stoic, and a Bob who keenly appreciates and readily acquires these qualities—both characters entirely larger than life.

Nevertheless, this nobility is achieved only by a great deal of auctorial editing of the characters, so that while larger-than-life they are both less than life-like. Yet this is apparently Birney's purpose, to give partial characterizations rather than real ones, to present a nature actively willful rather than passively indifferent, to employ celestial scale rather than terrestrial, to present young godlings rather than young men. And in these terms the poem is triumphant. Against a backdrop both magical and huge, David and Bob pursue their quest. Like a Canadian grail the Finger beckons them onward; like Galahad, David finds that success in this quest is also death, and again like Galahad accepts death calmly. Bob, his Lancelot, returns home guilt-ridden and repentant.

The chief weakness in "David," the melodrama in the final two sections, is in part a product of this guilt and of the excessive nobility of character. "No Bobby! Don't ever blame yourself. / I didn't test my foothold" (SP, 122), David lies to Bob as both vie for responsibility for the accident. Later Bob sententiously tells himself, "I knew / He had tested his holds. It was I who had not" (SP, 123). These passages contain, of course, the first serious feelings or issues faced by the two characters in the poem. The anomalous quality of the ending would seem to have much to do with the fact that Birney has suddenly attempted to plumb character in a poem which has to this point been a romance. In part nine, however, Birney returns us to the magic and danger of the natural world, "the purple glimmer of toadstools," "the spectral larches." And Bob can run on to the end of the legend he has lived—"the last of my youth, on the last of our mountains" (SP, 124).

The Damnation of Vancouver (1952-1957)

This play written for CBC radio in 1952 is Birney's
longest work in verse. Its subject is the question fundamental to Birney's humanism: can man shape for himself a significant and worthy future or must he die by
his own short-sightedness and greed? Its setting is a public hearing into the city of Vancouver's destiny. History
presides over the hearing; the future proposes Vancouver's imminent destruction, while the city through its
counsel attempts to parade its touristic and commercial
accomplishments. The play's structure is simple. There
are seven parts, the first expository and the remainder
presenting one each of the hearing's six witnesses. Four
of these witnesses, Captain George Vancouver, Chief
Skuh-watch-kwuh-tlath-kyutl, Gassy Jack Deighton, and
William Langland, are dead, being materialized by the
Minister of History for their assumed impartiality. The
other two are the geologist E. O. Seen and the irrepres-
sible housewife Mrs. Anyone.

Unlike "David," in which the principal element is the
setting, the core of "The Damnation of Vancouver" is its
ideas. Two overlapping conflicts dominate the play, both
of them common to Birney's other work. The first is between past and present, and again, as in the Latin American poems, it is oversimplified into a white and black
dichotomy. The second is between commercialism and
joy, the latter associated largely with the past and with
the character Mrs. Anyone, and the former with the
present. The chief spokesman for both the present and
commercialism is the city's counsel, Mr. P. S. (pseudo)
Legion, whose speech is a catalogue of Chamber of Com-

merce and Tourist Bureau clichés. Legion's name is "pseudo" because he represents in the play not true common man, like Mrs. Anyone, but the folksy capitalist who lives off common man by pretending to represent and serve him. His expulsion from our world late in the play by Mrs. Anyone and her own claiming of the name "Legion" symbolize Birney's old dream of mass-man's overthrowing of his hypocritical exploiters.

The past is celebrated by both Captain Vancouver and the Salish chieftain, whose recollections are particularly selective and sentimental—though apparently not intended as sentimental by Birney.

> . . . there were nights we returned from the mountains
> With deer on our shoulders,
> Or from the still coves with ducks.
> Then all the longhouse made music,
> There was roasting of spicy roots,
> There were sweet small plums,
> The green shoots of vines, and lily bulbs
> That grew for us unprompted.
> —It was not till *your* time, sir (*Turning* to LEGION),
> I saw a Salish go hungry. (*SP*, 178)

The attack on the baseness of Vancouver's "fast buck" culture is led by Langland and Gabriel Powers, the counsel for the future. Mrs. Anyone is the play's sole proponent of joy.

The play provides Birney with an opportunity for a dazzling display of technical virtuosity in a variety of verse styles. Each character, except the President, the Clerk of the Hearing, the stenographer, and Gassy Jack

Deighton, all of whom speak in prose, speaks in a verse matched to his personality. Captain Vancouver uses iambic pentameter couplets suitable to the rationalism of a late eighteenth-century gentleman. Chief Skuh-wath-kwuh-tlath-kyutl, who eulogizes the freedom and simplicity of native life, speaks in a highly rhetorical free verse which tends to echo years of oration in tribal council.

> My fathers, roaming ever eastward,
> Crossed Bering, made human half the world.
> Your fathers, whitening over Europe,
> And ever westering, circled back to us,
> Bringing us your woes, clasped in your totems,
> Carved in those Powers of lead and steel
> We had not known, unknowing had not lacked,
> Yet from the knowing needed. (SP, 176)

The ecologist, E. O. Seen, testifies in Anglo-Saxon alliterative verse patterns. Given the overwhelmingly elegiac and foreboding tone of extant Anglo-Saxon verse, these are a brilliant choice to convey the grim message the scientist must inevitably read from the indifferent rock.

> Then a sleek ball of ice, or of stone boiling.
> . . . .
> Life? Though man leap to Mars, he is lost in this fury.
> (SP, 187-188)

For Langland, Birney has recreated in modern English the syntax and mixed diction of the earlier poet's work, and captured the liquidity of his line.

> I fared then to a harbour where fish-heads floated,
> Saw longshoremen sweating and sailors aplenty,
> While a shipload of salesmen sailed to a convention
> Whiskeyed for the weekend—and their wenches with
> them.
>
> (SP, 200)

The verse of the two opposing counsels is as skillfully designed as any in the play. That of Gabriel Powers is of variable metre but is dominated by ambiguous Joycean puns through which Powers can convey the menacingly enigmatic nature of both past and impending events.

> From the ash of the fir springs the fire-weed;
> From the ask of his faring your fear.
> His village did not die that Legion's might
> More losty lift, but that you might be meek
> To understay your own swift Inding. (SP, 183)

That of Legion is the doggerel of the ad-man, and is uttered with the assurance of a limited mind that completely believes its own clichés.

> Is this Stanley Park! Really, Mr. Minister,
> The motives of this witness are definitely sinister.
> The picknickers' mecca, the boaters' dream,
> Alpine vistas, and tea with cream!
> Why this is where our cityfolk release all their
> tensions!
>
> (SP, 201)

Only the verse given to Mrs. Anyone, the crucial character of the play, is inadequate. She is billed as "a mere living housewife" (SP, 204), and by her name presented as Vancouver's representative woman. Yet her verse can be painfully formal, pedantically complicated, or overtly rhetorical.

> Whether the record mutes me,
> Or my child unloose me to sorrow,
> Whether the glaciers glide,
> Or the sun scream down tomorrow—
> I woke today with my husband,
> To the bronze clashing of peaks,
> To the long shout of the ocean,
> And the blood alive in my cheeks. (*SP*, 205)

Birney has obviously intended her as an exuberant, garrulous person, but he has given her verse so openly contrived that he has put both her authenticity and spontaneity into question. There is no way that she can be accepted as a common housewife. Birney's carelessness here seriously mars the play since the resolution of its action—the common man's reclamation of his right to participate in his culture's destiny—is based entirely on her authenticity.

Throughout the play's course the evidence of the witnesses unfailingly constructs Vancouver's image as a corrupt, development-crazed, and environment-destroying city. Both Captain Vancouver and Gassy Jack Deighton recall the pure waters of the inlet that have now been permanently fouled, and, in contrasting ways, recall the virtues of the Indian peoples that the white man has displaced and destroyed. Deighton castigates the "landsharks" who have cared only for the money they could extract from the city's soil. Langland condemns the en-

101

tire city as a collection of soulless and animalistic worshippers of Lady Meed.

> Beyond the tamed shores that no tide cleansed
> Rose the raped mountains, scarred with fire and
>   finance,
> And raddled with the lonely roofs of the rich,
> Of barristers and bookies and brokers aplenty
> Of agents for septic tanks, for aspirin, or souls.
> Executives, crooners, con-men a few— (SP, 200)

And throughout, Legion naïvely abets the prosecution by arguing with rather than cross-examining the witnesses, by bragging about the city's "houses of tomorrow," her "visiting Shriners," her "helicopter-jet port," and by proclaiming such inanities as "You can't have industry and keep your sky blue." Mrs. Anyone's task is to overcome all this evidence strictly by the strength of her joy in living and her faith in the will of man to save rather than despoil his world. After disposing of Legion, she disarms Powers, who represents in the play the immense uncertainty of the forces which dog our separate and collective fates, by proclaiming Birney's basic humanistic doctrine that man's future will be what man makes it: "I am mistress over you, my master Powers." Just as man admittedly has chosen to date to be a spiritual failure in Vancouver, she tells Powers, so too he has the power to choose whatever he will for the future.

> Till sun sears we make him sire us.
> Till then all shapes and sounds will fire us,
> Our thinkers knit them and our artists net. (SP, 211)

Her argument is sound, and based on it the play's ending, intellectually at least, is secure. It is only Mrs. Anyone as a character who does not convince; she is neither Mrs. Anyone nor Mrs. Legion; her language is not anyone's; her logic is not anyone's. Thus while we can accept here Birney's philosophy, our trust in his knowledge of mankind is dangerously shaken by his strange concept of "mere" woman.

Nevertheless, "The Damnation of Vancouver" is an excellent play and a virtuoso work of poetry. As in *Turvey* and *Down the Long Table*, though the overall concept of the work can be faulted, the quality of the writing line by line seldom can. "The Damnation" is also the fullest and most effective statement by Birney of his humanism, incorporating not only his hope for mankind but also his other major themes—his sense of nature's mechanicality and man's impermanence, his romantic view of America's native peoples, and detestation of materialism, hucksterism, and ignorance. In addition, it gives us again Birney the myth-maker, constructing both an idyllic Indian Vancouver of the past and a utopian city of the future where Mrs. Anyone can see "selfless deeds . . . multiply / And hum like simmering bees across my city's gardens" (*SP*, 212).

NOVEMBER WALK NEAR FALSE CREEK MOUTH (1963)

The third of Birney's long poems is also about the destruction of Vancouver. And again the city faces this destruction from atomic weapons, the horror of which has haunted Birney since 1945. In that year he wrote two Housmanesque pieces about the newly designed bomb, and foresaw even then in "the atom's terror" ("Time Bomb," *NIT*, 6), the likelihood of "a world of bone" ("Each Lie," *SP*, 150). In "The Damnation of Vancouver," although Powers informs the hearing that "the Veedails of the dooming . . . are not yet warred out foully" (*SP*, 166), and later that the "method of bomb-nation's not yet subtled," Birney never allows Legion's guess that the city may be "Blown up? Blown down? H-bombed?! Zee-bopped?!" (*SP*, 172) to be directly contradicted. During the late fifties and early sixties Birney writes a number of sober articles about the possibility of man's atomic extinction—"The Writer and the H-Bomb,"[2] "The Modern Face of Hubris,"[3] "The Pride Before the Fall-out,"[4] "Random Remarks on a Random World."[5] In these, his feelings about man's chances are still ambivalent: the bomb may be fated to fall but meanwhile it is man's nature to continue the attempt to avert the holocaust. By the time of the writing of "November Walk," however, Birney's humanism has failed and his pessimism about man's future grown complete; hence the opening lines:

> *The time is the last of warmth*
> *and the fading of brightness*
> > *before the final flash and the night* (*SP*, 133).

Throughout the poem Birney sees his fellow citizens engaged in "the separate wait / for the mass dying" (*SP*, 135) and resigned to the imminence of "the unimaginable brightness" (*SP*, 133).

> At this edge of the blast
> a young girl sits on a granite bench

so still as if already only
silhouette burned in the stone (*SP*, 136).

At the same time Birney's sense of Vancouver's corruption has increased over that evident in "The Damnation."
He no longer troubles to document a case against the city;
instead he labels it with gratuitous and derogatory adjectives: "barren," "faded," "ashen," "compulsive," "shapeless," "gasping," "spilling," "bland," "aseptic." Apparently
the city is no longer sufficiently significant to warrant
energetic vituperation.

At the heart of "November Walk" are the late-autumn
season and the sunset that Birney watches from the English Bay beach during the meditations that form the
poem. He seizes upon both of these as specific indicators
of the doom that awaits mankind. The chilly and nearly
deserted beach suggests to him the languor of a race that
has ceased trying to survive; the sunset suggests the
radiant light of an inevitable atomic war. Most of the
craft of the poem is devoted to Birney's attempt to force
this interpretation on the autumnal sunset. Many of the
adjectives of the poem are openly argumentative in that
they assume conditions undocumented within the poem.
Thus the "world of lungs" is termed "gasping," "nations"
are termed "stranded," the descendants of King Alfred
are said to be "sighing like old pines." Other adjectives
are used to make unavoidable qualities seem somehow
reprehensible; the city is called "mortal," scows called
"mute." Many of the images of the poem seem similarly
heavy-handed—"the children's pool waiting like faith /
for summer" (*SP*, 140); "pylons marching over the peaks
/ of mountains without Olympus" (*SP*, 141). Twenty

years before in "Laurentian Shield" (SA, 11-12) Birney accepted a "heavenless" world; it seems unworthy of him to recriminate here.

Birney also uses to support his pessimistic vision the same white and black dichotomy between past and present that we have seen him use in other poems—as is evident in the "Olympus" passage above. A variety of aspects of the past is lamented in this way. There is more Greek theogony:

> and none ever heard
> the horn of Triton or merman (SP, 137).

There is Hebrew myth:

> a troller perhaps   lies longdrowned
> on an Arrarat [sic] of broken clamshells
> and the flakings of dead crabs (SP, 140).

There is Christianity:

> . . . this wrinkled triad of tourists
> .   .   .   .
>
> seeking a starred sign for the bus-stop
> They dangle plastic totems   a kewpie
> a Hong Kong puzzle for somebody's child
> who waits to be worshipped
> back on the prairie farm (SP, 134).

There is Teutonic mythology, now unaware of itself and living out its days in Winnipeg:

Not the Lockeys of *Out*garden surely
I said   *Yes*   she said   but I live
in Winnipeg now   Why for heaven's *sake*
I said   then you *must* know Carl *Thor*son?

(SP, 136).

There is the "local Buddha" (SP, 135), asleep on a park bench. And from "The Damnation of Vancouver" come Birney's idealized Indian tribes:

> . . . in the clotting air by a shore
> where shamans never again will sound
> with moon-snail conch the ritual plea
> to brother salmon or vanished seal (SP, 137).

Here, then, is the "twilight of the gods," of all gods. But unlike the Norse *Gotterdammerung*, this twilight of baleful omens sees as yet no violence, no energy of plot and counterplot. All gods are debased and moribund, and the people await the last explosion with languorous acquiescence.

In its language the poem is greatly overburdened with adjectives, particularly with participials. As this tendency indicates, the poem is overwhelmingly descriptive, and contains little action, motion, or excitement. It possesses the same languor that Birney finds culpable in the people of the poem, but, while this congruence of mood may be theoretically desirable, the result is weak art. The poem's three most frequent verbs are *to be, to sit,* and *to wait.* The remainder are dominated by *walk, come, lie, stray, stare, crawl, wander, cling, slip,* and *nudge*—not an energetic group. Moved by these, "November Walk" is a poem of regret and resignation by a poet ostensibly as dejected and moribund as his fellow citizens.

In structure the poem is clearly meant to have organic form. There is no preconceived structural plan evident; Birney seems to have wanted the personal meditation to find its own course. It is, however, no work of projective verse. The poet seems uneasy in the form, and, perhaps because of his years of impersonal and highly thematic verse, unsure of his voice. He inserts italicized onomato-poetic passages at irregular intervals which interrupt the meditation and insist upon the poem's intended mes-sage.

> *The beat is the small   slap   slapping*
> *of the tide sloping   slipping*
> *its long soft fingers into the tense*
> *joints of the trapped seawall* (SP, 133)

In many of these passages the open artificiality of the verse makes both the message and poem seem strained. The dominantly adjectival quality of the poem both reinforces the impression that the poet is trying too hard and dulls any sense of perceptual accuracy. In addition Birney seems to lapse at times into Anglo-Saxon verse lines.

> Nor for certain the gamey old gaffer
> asleep on the bench like a local Buddha (SP, 135)

In this example neither the stale colloquialism nor the verse form contributes to an authenticity of voice.

"November Walk" is an unusual poem for Birney, and certainly not one of his best. In form it attempts to be open, but in theme it is closed from its beginning, and this closure tends to paralyze the form. Nothing can really happen in the poem because, while leaving the form open, Birney has preconceived what the poem will "say." The opening lines tell us about our atomic doom; the remainder embroider but do not advance. Birney seems to have come to both the personal lyric and the projective form too late to be consistently successful. The shorter "A Walk in Kyoto" is a triumph, but "November Walk" is paralyzed by his old proselytizing habits.

Yet this paralysis is not without additional explanation. We have seen how Birney's humanism from the beginning of his career motivated and energized his work. "November Walk" is the poem in which this optimistic humanism dies. The death is evident in the verbs of the poem, in how the old verbs of violence, toil, and aspiration have been replaced by verbs of stasis and slow motion. It is evident in the view of nature, no longer "glittering," "clashing," "soaring," or "shouting," but now "sludged" and "doomed." It is also apparent in two despairing images of the poem in which man's failure to realize his dreams or attain Spender's sun are subtly symbolized.

> . . . I walk as the waves stream
> from my feet to the bay to the far shore
> Where they lap like dreams that never reach
>
> The tree-barbed tip of Point Grey's lance
> has failed again to impale the gone sun (*SP*, 139)

There is no Mrs. Anyone in "November Walk" to pro-
claim her joy in living. There is no small boy to fly his
monstrous kite "higher into the endless winds of the
world" ("A Walk in Kyoto," SP, 11). Birney makes no
mythology take root in its measures, not even his myth
of indifferent but dynamic nature. With the gods dying,
the myths of the past can enter the poem only to de-
monstrate their absence in the present. Ararat turns to
broken clamshells; there are "antennae above the crosses"
(SP, 141); Mycenae stands only as a symbol of death
for both itself and the other city with a Lions' Gate.

> At the edge of knowledge the *Prince Apollo*
>   (or is it the *Princess Helen*?)
> floats in a paperblue fusion of air
> gulf   Mykenean islands
> and crawls with its freight of flesh
> toward the glare and the night waiting
> behind the hidden Gate of the Lions (SP, 137)

Everything else typical of a Birney poem is evident, the
romantic view of the past, the hatred of sterile life patterns and commercial exploitation, but his tenacious
optimism, and its likely corollary, his vigour and sure-
ness of language, are totally lacking.

THE MAMMOTH CORRIDORS (1965)

In "The Mammoth Corridors" Birney returns to the
Rocky Mountains, the setting of his first long poem,
"David," and abandons the many intransitive verbs and
negative-quality adjectives ("shapeless," "barren," "bland")

of "November Walk." The scenes of the poem discourage hope for human accomplishment as effectively as those of "November Walk," but their language is energetic, as if Birney has gone beyond despair in his knowledge that the earth's future may not include humanity.

> Over the taut bridge   through the lonely park
> my wheels will themselves to the shrieking
> (RBS, [11])

The people of this poem are small, vigorous, limited, and doomed. The most vigorous, the first white settlers of British Columbia, are limited by their shallowness and greed.

> . . . those first compulsive whites   the Searchers
> for gold   absolution   furs   or mere difference
> came hurtling in improbable canoes   heavy with
>   liquor
> and fear   bearing their beads and syphilis
> muzzleloaders and god (RBS, [12])

The least vigorous, Birney's contemporaries, at least twitch nervously through their routines.

> Then the spastic traffic
> of buyers and bought   pedlars of weed and soap
> of acid and snow   of work and wonder   in
>   Skidrow's lanes (RBS, [11])

In "November Walk" Birney's own sharing of man's apathy and helplessness was implicit in the poem's weak

111

vocabulary and monotonous rhythms. Here he explicitly but energetically names himself one of the failing and degenerate race, powerless in face of the inexorable forces of nature.

> from my own lusts and neckties and novels
> from ulcers vitamins bulletins *accidia*
> i lie unshielded under each night's motel roof
> <div align="right">(<i>RBS</i>, [12])</div>

Even the landscape in this poem is subject to limits and decay. Whereas in "David" the mountains were eternal and knowledgeable, here they too are subject to time and process. As the poem begins "the great islands" of the British Columbia coast are "drowning in the morning's waves from Asia" (*RBS*, [11]). To the east Birney finds "tortured peaks," "the blind dive of the canyons," "ice-bitten ranges," and "gouged hills" from glaciation (*RBS*, [12-13]). These mountains dwarf man in size, age, and durability.

> the tortured peaks only a breath more broken
> the blind dive of the canyons a scratch of a century
>   deeper
> since those first compulsive whites . . . (*RBS*, [12])

But they are themselves dwarfed and "broken" by process, and will eventually succumb to the future's ice ages. Once the land was to Birney synonymous with nature; now, in his growing pessimism, he appears emotionally convinced of E. O. Seen's realistic view of the planet as being at the mercy of cosmic fate.

Thus "The Mammoth Corridors" is the least humanistic of Birney's poems. It tells us that the only virtue
man has ever had is his participation in process. The first
North Americans had this virtue, but modern man has
never even sought it.

> Surviving westward then over howling summits
> to possess these still fresh-hewn alps
> (which I inheriting do not possess)
> moving by day through bear and elk and by their
>   killing
> outliving sleep by capturing the deer's Wit
> the Power of cougar   in nets of dance and word
> (RBS, [13])

The modern lacks all dignity.

> An ash of ice whines at the crosses of streets
> A morning drunk is spattering curses
> over a halfbreed girl in a blotched doorway
> (RBS, [14])

His superficiality and short-sighted materialism are heavi-
ly underlined by Birney in "quotations" from an apocry-
phal tourist guidebook which he uses throughout to
parallel and counterpoint his own observations.

> . . . miles of towering Rockies—tracing in reverse the
> spectacular route taken by British Columbia's first ex-
> plorers and hardy traders. Convenient to the trans-
> continental railways this four-lane freeway offers
> American visitors every modern . . . (RBS, [12])

Yet Birney here (unlike in "November Walk") can look at uncaring nature and her processes with both equanimity and admiration. Man may be doomed, but at least now he lives. His life and his world have been made by the very forces which damn him.

> Eastward again I am pulled to a sky
> of land flattened white to the Pole and
> drawn against the unstillable winds
> the breath of that madcap virgin mother of ice
> who embraced it all a wink ago in the world's eye
>
> (*RBS*, [14])

And that virgin herself will bring, as seen before, three things which have always eluded man—love, silence, "a long hard peace" (*RBS*, [14]).

"The Mammoth Corridors" is a powerful and convincing poem, the strongest and most ambitious of *Rag and Bone Shop*. Birney's late-acquired equanimity in the face of man's apparently finite destiny enables him to concentrate on the energy of natural process rather than on the human paralysis he believes this process has caused. As a result his images are sharp and evocative.

> trailing the great woolly ones
> watching the gleam of nine-foot tusks
> tracking   floundering in the newborn earth
> wolving by the black rivers that rattled from the glare
> of the narrowing icewalls (*RBS*, [13])

This equanimity also clarifies the rational structure of

the poem, helping the poet to avoid the meditative floundering of "November Walk." In "The Mammoth Corridors" Birney's perspective on natural event is clear and far-ranging; his vision of humanity is firm and consistent. His pretense of quoting from a tourist guidebook gives the poem an apparent documentary core to testify to the accuracy of the poet's vision of man. The guidebook, in fact, has the appearance of determining the course of the poem, leading Birney to the "Arctic conditions" and his realization of the planet's chilling future.

Throughout, the poem has a tone of complete authenticity; not only are the guidebook quotations convincingly realistic, but Birney's own observations seem accurate and impartial. In "November Walk" his attempts to make reality appear sordid and hopeless were often obviously argumentative. Here the details he observes—"cherry petals on the slick streets," "howling summits," "the blind dive of the canyons"—ring so true that they obviate any need for argument.

No final estimate of Earle Birney can be made at this time, for he is still writing and publishing, and, considering the resourcefulness and versatility he has already shown, could provide any number of surprises. A few things can be established or predicted, however. Birney is certainly the most accomplished technician of poetry ever to write in Canada, and likely will be remembered for this above all else. His poems will outrank his novels in importance, and of these "The Damnation of Vancouver" should eventually be recognized as his important and characteristic work, replacing in this respect the hurriedly canonized "David." For "The Damnation" not only contains the greatest evidence of his technical virtuosity but also gives the fullest expression of his romanticism and humanism.

Especially for his exuberant variety Birney will be remembered above his Canadian contemporaries. When one considers the conservative verse forms and impersonality of Smith, the alluvial impressionism of Souster, the wit of Scott, or even the accomplished and lyrical life-force verse of Layton, one quickly becomes aware of the extensive range of Birney's achievement. His "David" and "The Damnation of Vancouver" are both more carefully written than Pratt's long poems. His Latin American and Far East poems are without equal in their scrupulous and sensitive attention to the place visited and in their masterful use of dialogue. Also without equal are those products of his anomalous background, his combination of learning and humour, of intellectual pride and proletarian sympathy, of woodscraft and humanism, of satire and romance. And finally there is Birney's humanism spanning a range from a dream of a global man-centered society to a sincere love of the most obscure individual. While F. R. Scott's humanism is largely negative, expressed in irony and humour, and Pratt's chiefly an extolling of subservience to church, tribe, race, country, corporation, machine, or military necessity, Birney celebrates the richness of an individual joy that must go on from Bankok to Vancouver, in spite of totalitarian oppression, commercial greed, or the threat of atomic doom, if human life is to continue to have value.

Throughout the main body of this survey of Birney's work there has been little attempt to judge him in relation to his fellow writers, for relative judgements tell us little that is specific about the work itself. In addition, the specialized interests and talents of Canadian poets make grounds for comparison between them few and shaky. It must be observed, however, that Birney has written well across a much broader range of verse than have any of his countrymen. A very large number of Birney's works, some impersonal and some personal, some romantic and some satirical, are classics of Canadian poetry: "David," "Vancouver Lights," "Dusk on the Bay," "The Road to Nijmegen," "Anglosaxon Street," "The Damnation of Vancouver," "The Bear on the Delhi Road," "A Walk in Kyoto," and latterly "Charité, Espérance, et Foi." Throughout these he has attempted to bring myth, hope, and maturity to his "heavenless" country. Although he began writing relatively late and continued only fitfully, what Birney has written proves him to be one of our most talented, conscientious, and versatile poets, if not to date our greatest.

NOTES

NOTES TO CHAPTER ONE

[1] Tape-recorded interview by Frank Davey, Montreal, 26 Oct. 1969.

[2] "'Pen' Review," manuscript held by the University of Toronto Library, Birney Collection.

[3] "On Proletarian Literature," *The Link*, I, #3 [1937].

[4] Feb. 1937, p. 24.

[5] "Poet Without a Muse," *Canadian Literature*, 30 (Autumn 1966), 14-20.

[6] *The Canadian Forum*, April 1941, p. 28.

[7] "Poetry, 1935-1950," in Klinck *et al.* (ed.), *Literary History of Canada*, p. 762.

[8] Interview by Rex Frost, CFRB radio (Toronto), June 1946. Typed transcript in University of Toronto Birney Collection.

[9] "Age Shall Not Wither Thee," *Here and Now*, 1 (Jan. 1949), 86-87.

[10] *Canadian Home Journal*, July 1948.

[11] *Saturday Night*, LXX (20 Aug. 1955), 27-28.

[12] CBC radio, 1952. Published in *The Canadian Library Association Bulletin*, IX (Nov. 1952), 77-79.

[13] "Lake O'Hara" (photographic print with text), Standard Oil Company of B.C., n.d., in the University of Toronto Birney Collection.

[14] Tape-recorded interview, Ameliasburg, Ontario, 2-9 Feb. 1968.

[15] Tape-recorded interview, York University, Toronto, 8 Feb. 1968.

[16] "Poet Without a Muse," p. 14.

[17]Birney's personal copies of his early books, most of these studded with notes, comments, and revisions, are in the University of Toronto Birney Collection.

[18]"Creative Writing and Destructive Living," paper delivered to Humanities Conference, Reed College, Oregon, 1954. Manuscript in University of Toronto Birney Collection.

Notes to Chapter Two

[1]"Introduction," *Turvey* (Toronto: McClelland and Stewart, 1963), p. xv.

[2]"Turvey and the Critics," *Canadian Literature*, 30 (Autumn 1966), 24-25.

[3]"Introduction," pp. xiv-xv.

[4]*Ten Canadian Poets* (Toronto: Ryerson, 1958), p. 324.

[5]*Ibid.*, p. 325.

Notes to Chapter Three

[1]*Ten Canadian Poets*, p. 304.

[2]*Ibid.*, p. 326.

[3]*Ibid.*, p. 295.

[4]*Ibid.*, p. 296.

[5]Previously "senor"; correction requested by McClelland and Stewart.

[6]Previously "Sestina for Tehuantepec"; correction requested by McClelland and Stewart.

[7]Previously "Pizarro"; correction requested by McClelland and Stewart.

[8]"Canadian Poetry?" *Tamarack Review*, 29 (Autumn 1963), 72.

[9]Leon Trotsky, in an interview with Earle Birney,

Hoenefoss, Norway, November 1935. Manuscript "Further Conversations with L. T.," University of Toronto Birney Collection, p. 1.

[10]Interview, 26 Oct. 1969.

[11]"Earle Birney and the Compound Ghost," *Canadian Literature*, 13 (Summer 1962), 5-14.

[12]Birney's notes in personal copy of *David*, University of Toronto Birney Collection.

[13]*Ten Canadian Poets*, p. 305.

[14]Previously "Romeros"; correction requested by McClelland and Stewart.

NOTES TO CHAPTER FOUR

[1]*Ten Canadian Poets*, p. 306.

[2]*Queen's Quarterly*, LXII (Spring 1955), 37-44.

[3]In J. Alan Ross (ed.), *Hubris, Man and Education* (Bellingham, Washington, Union Printing Co., 1959), pp. 46-60.

[4]Manuscript in University of Toronto Birney Collection. Marginal note indicates that Birney delivered this paper as a sermon in the Unitarian Church, Vancouver, Summer 1960. Text is an alternate rendering of "The Modern Face of Hubris."

[5]*The Western Humanities Review*, XV:1 (Winter 1961), 3-10.

BIBLIOGRAPHY

A. Books by Birney

I. Poetry

David and Other Poems. Toronto: Ryerson, 1942.

Ice Cod Bell or Stone. Toronto: McClelland and Stewart, 1962.

Memory No Servant. Trumansburg, New York: New Books, 1968.

Near False Creek Mouth. Toronto: McClelland and Stewart, 1964.

Now Is Time. Toronto: Ryerson, 1945.

Pnomes Jukollages and other Stunzas (*Gronk* 3, series 4). [Toronto, 1969].

The Poems of Earle Birney. Toronto: McClelland and Stewart, 1969.

Rag and Bone Shop. Toronto: McClelland and Stewart, 1971.

Selected Poems. Toronto: McClelland and Stewart, 1966.

The Strait of Anian. Toronto: Ryerson, 1948.

Trial of a City and Other Verse. Toronto: Ryerson, 1952.

II. Novels

Down the Long Table. Toronto: McClelland and Stewart, 1955.

———. London: Abelard-Schuman, 1959.

The Kootenay Highlander. Pirated edition of *Turvey.* London: Four Square Books, 1960.

Turvey. Toronto: McClelland and Stewart, 1949.

———. Toronto: Collins, 1952.

———. London and New York: Abelard-Schuman, 1959.

———. Toronto: McClelland and Stewart, New Canadian Library, 1963.

III. CRITICISM

Chaucer's Irony. Diss. University of Toronto, 1936.
The Creative Writer. Toronto: CBC Publications, 1966.

IV. EDITIONS

Twentieth-Century Canadian Poetry. Toronto: Ryerson, 1953.
Record of Service in the Second World War. A supplement to the University of B.C. War Memorial Manuscript Record. Vancouver: UBC, 1955.
New Voices. Joint editor of Canadian university writing in 1956 with Ira Dilworth, Desmond Pacey, Jean-Charles Bonenfant, and Roger Duhamel. Toronto and Vancouver: Dent, 1956.
Selected Poems of Malcolm Lowry. San Francisco: City Lights, 1962.
Lunar Caustic, by Malcolm Lowry. Joint editor with Margerie Lowry. London: Cape, 1968.

V. PAMPHLETS

Canada Calling. Montreal: CBC International Service, 1946.
Conversations with Trotsky. London: privately printed, 1936, under pseudonym E. Robertson. University of Toronto Birney collection includes unpublished MS. appendix "Further Conversations with L.T."
Convocation Address. Calgary: University of Alberta, 1965.

B. Short Stories by Birney

"Bird in the Bush," *Mademoiselle*, May 1948, pp. 143, 236-239.

"Enigma in Ebony," *Maclean's*, 15 Oct. 1953, pp. 16-17, 104, 106-108.

"The Levin Bolt," *Canadian Life*, 1 (March-April 1949), 7, 31, 38; as "A London Sketch," in Ralph Gustafson, ed., *Canadian Accent* (London: Penguin, 1951).

"Mickey was a Swell Guy," *National Home Monthly*, 49 (Nov. 1948), 16-17, 26-27.

"Private Turvey Becomes Acting Senior Officer," in John Robins, ed., *A Book of Canadian Humour* (Toronto: Ryerson, 1951), pp. 49-56; in George E. Nelson, ed., *Northern Lights* (New York: Doubleday, 1960), pp. 333-339.

"The Reverend Eastham Discovers Life," *The Ubyssey*, annual literary supplement, March 1924, n.p.

"The Strange Smile of Thos. Turvey," *Here and Now*, 2 (June 1949), 38-45.

"Turvey Engages a Paratrooper," *Saturday Night*, 64 (9 Aug. 1949), 21.

"What's This Agoosto," *Montreal Standard*, 29 July 1950, pp. 14-15, 21.

C. Selected Articles and Addresses by Birney

"'After His Ymage'—The Central Ironies of the Friar's Tale," *Mediaeval Studies*, XXI (1959), 17-35.

"Age Shall Not Wither Thee," *Here and Now*, 1 (Jan. 1949), 86-87. Extracts from Birney's letter of resignation from the Canadian Authors Association.

"A.J.M.S.," *Canadian Literature*, 15 (Winter 1963), 4-6.

"Aldous Huxley," in Pelham Edgar, ed., *The Art of the Novel* (New York: Macmillan, 1933), pp. 280-290.

"Another Month," *The Canadian Forum,* XVI (Feb. 1937), 24, one of a series of columns under pseudonym "Rufus."

"The B.C. Centennial," *The Canadian Forum* XXXVIII (1958), 6-8.

"The Beginnings of Chaucer's Irony," *PMLA* 54 (1939), 637-655.

"Britanny, In and Out of the Guide Books," *Saturday Night,* 68 (8 Aug. 1953), 14.

"Canada and World Politics," *New International,* Sept. 1938, pp. 261-264, under pseudonym E. Robertson.

"The Canadian Writer vs the Canadian Education," *Evidence,* 10 (1967), 97-113.

"Chaucer's 'Gentil' Manciple and his 'Gentil' Tale," *Neuphilologische Mitteilungen,* LXI:3, 257-267.

"Creative Writing and Destructive Living," paper delivered to Humanities Conference, Reed College, Ore., 1954.

"E. J. Pratt and his Critics," in Robert L. MacDougall, ed., *Our Living Tradition, Second and Third Series* (Toronto: University of Toronto Press, 1959), pp. 123-147.

"English Irony Before Chaucer," *University of Toronto Quarterly,* VI (1937), 538-557.

"Fiction of James T. Farrell," *The Canadian Forum,* XIX (1939), 21-24.

"Has Poetry a Future in Canada?" *Manitoba Arts Review,* 5 (Spring 1946), 7-15.

"The Importance of Being Ernest Hemingway," *The Canadian Forum,* XVI (1937), 322-323.

"The Inhibited and the Uninhibited: Ironic Structure in the 'Miller's Tale'," *Neophilologus*, XLIV (1960), 333-338.

"Is Chaucer's Irony a Modern Discovery?" *Journal of English and Germanic Philology*, XLI (1942), 303-319.

"Is French-Canada Going Fascist?" *New International*, Oct. 1938, pp. 304-307, under pseudonym E. Robertson.

"Lake O'Hara," text for photographic print, Standard Oil Company of British Columbia, n.d.

"Mexico in One Jump," *Saturday Night*, 70 (20 Aug. 1955), 27-28.

"The Modern Face of Hubris," in J. Alan Ross, ed., *Hubris, Man, and Education* (Bellingham, Wash.: Union Printing Co., 1959), pp. 46-60.

"On Being a Canadian Author," CBC radio, 1952; published in *The Canadian Library Association Bulletin*, 9 (Nov. 1952), 77-79.

"On Proletarian Literature," *The Link*, I:3 ([1937]), 2.

" 'Pen' Review," unpublished book review of *Pen*, University of Utah student literary magazine, [1934].

"Personal Experiences in Nazi Germany," *New Leader*, 13 Dec. 1935.

"Poetry is an Oral Art; Poet Should Hire Hall," *Toronto Globe and Mail*, 22 June 1949, p. 9.

"Poets and Painters: Rivals or Partners?" *Canadian Art*, 14 (Summer 1957), 148-150.

"The Pride Before the Fallout," sermon delivered at Unitarian Church, Vancouver, Summer 1950. Alternate rendering of "The Modern Face of Hubris."

"Proletarian Literature: Theory and Practice," *The Canadian Forum*, XVII (May 1937), 58-60.

"Random Remarks on a Random World," *Humanities Association Bulletin,* XXIX (1960), 10-11, 18-20; *Western Humanities Review,* XV (1961), 3-10.

"Reminiscences of Birney's Two Years as Editor of *Canadian Poetry Magazine,*" *The Canadian Author and Bookman,* 39 (Winter 1963), 4-6.

Review of Gertrude Stein's *Ida, The Canadian Forum,* XXI (1941), 28.

"Sherwood Anderson: A Memory," *The Canadian Forum,* XXI (1941), 82-83.

"Structural Irony within the 'Summoner's Tale'," *Anglia,* LXXVIII (1960), 204-218.

"Swan Song," *The Canadian Forum,* XVI (Jan. 1937), 23-24, review of A. E. Housman's *More Poems.*

"To Arms with Canadian Poetry," *The Canadian Forum,* XIX (1940), 322-324.

"*Turvey* and the Critics," *Canadian Literature,* 30 (Autumn 1966), 21-25.

"The Two William Faulkners," *The Canadian Forum,* XVIII (1938), 84-85.

"The Two Worlds of Geoffrey Chaucer," *Manitoba Arts Review,* 2 (Winter 1941), 3-16.

"The Unknown Poetry of Malcolm Lowry," *The British Columbia Library Quarterly,* 24 (April 1961), 33-40.

"Utah Students See for Themselves," *The Student Review,* 3 (Feb. 1934), 22-24, under pseudonym David Brownstone.

"War and the English Intellectuals," *The Canadian Forum,* XXI (1941), 110-114.

"The Writer and the H-Bomb," *Queen's Quarterly,* LXII (1955), 37-44.

"Yes, Canadians Can Read—But Do They?" *Canadian Home Journal*, July 1948.

D. Interviews with Birney

Davey, Frank. Toronto, 26 Oct. 1969. Tape-recording is in Mr. Davey's private possession.

Evans, Merilyn. Toronto, 8 Feb. 1968. Tape-recording is in Al Purdy's private possession.

Frost, Rex. Toronto, CFRB radio, June 1946. Typed transcript is in the University of Toronto Library, Birney collection.

Purdy, Al. Ameliasburg, 2-8 Feb. 1968. Tape-recording is in Mr. Purdy's private possession.

E. Selected Criticism

Beattie, Munro. "Poetry (1935-1950)," in Carl F. Klinck, ed., *Literary History of Canada* (Toronto: University of Toronto Press, 1965), pp. 761-765.

Bonenfant, Jean-Charles. L'influence de la litterature canadienne-anglaise au Canada français," *Culture*, 17 (1956), 251-260.

Brown, E. K. *On Canadian Poetry*. Toronto: Ryerson, 1943, pp. 76-78.

Clay, Charles. "Earle Birney," in W. P. Percival, ed., *Leading Canadian Poets* (Toronto: Ryerson, 1948), pp. 23-29.

Colombo, John Robert. "Poetic Ambassador," *Canadian Literature*, 24 (Spring 1965), 55-59.

Daniells, Roy. "Earle Birney et Robert Finch," *Gants du Ciel*, XI (1946), 83-96.

Dooley, D. J. "The Satiric Novel in Canada Today," *Queen's Quarterly*, LXIV (1958), 576-590.

Fredeman, W. E. "Earle Birney: Poet," *The British Columbia Library Quarterly*, XXIII (1960), 8-15.

Noel-Bentley, Peter C. *A Study of the Poetry of Earle Birney*. Unpublished M.A. thesis, University of Toronto, 1966.

Pacey, Desmond. *Creative Writing in Canada*. Toronto: Ryerson, 1961, pp. 150-153.

———. *Ten Canadian Poets*. Toronto: Ryerson, 1958, pp. 293-326.

Phelps, Arthur L. *Canadian Writers*. Toronto: McClelland and Stewart, 1951, pp. 111-119.

Skelton, Robin. "Canadian Poetry?" *Tamarack Review* 29, (Autumn 1963), 71-82.

Smith, A. J. M. "A Unified Personality," *Canadian Literature*, 30 (Autumn 1966), 2-13.

Wells, Henry W. *Where Poetry Stands Now*. Toronto: Ryerson, 1948, pp. 18-19, 79.

West, Paul. "Earle Birney and the Compound Ghost," *Canadian Literature*, 13 (Summer 1962), 5-14.

Wilson, Milton. "Poet Without a Muse," *Canadian Literature*, 30 (Autumn 1966), 14-20.

Woodcock, George. "Introduction," in Earle Birney, *Turvey* (Toronto: McClelland and Stewart, New Canadian Library, 1963), pp. ix-xv.

———. "Turning New Leaves," *The Canadian Forum*, XLVI (1966), 115-116.

F. BIBLIOGRAPHICAL INFORMATION

Noel-Bentley, Peter C. "Earle Birney: a Bibliography in Progress, 1923-1969," *West Coast Review*, V:2 (Oct. 1970), 45-53.